STANLEY MARON

KIBBUTZ IN A MARKET SOCIETY

YAD TABENKIN

Editor: Shimon Mahler

Typesetting: **Ilana Bernstein**

© **1993**

All rights reserved by Yad Tabenkin

P.O. Ramat Efal

52960 Israel

ISBN 965 282 041-5

Printed in Israel

TABLE OF CONTENTS

INTRODUCTION

"Kibbutz" is the Hebrew name of a communal settlement based on the principle of a shared home for a large number of individuals and families. The first kibbutz was founded in 1910, and by 1991 there were 270 legally recognized kibbutzim (plural form), with a total population of 129,300. Most individual kibbutzim have a population of 300 to 600 persons, though the largest have well over a thousand.

The communal dining hall is the center of communal life and symbolizes the predominance of communal consumption. All buildings and means of production are communally owned, and all economic activities are communally operated. Most members work within the communal territory, and most of the work is done by the kibbutz members themselves both for reasons of principle and efficiency. Labor is regarded as having a value of its own that cannot be translated into sums of money. Members do not receive wages. They engage in the economic functions of the kibbutz as participant-owners for whom wage incentives are not required in order to achieve a high standard of efficiency. All communal consumption is also liberated from market conditions, just as it is in any private home. For more individual needs and wants, those based on private choice, members receive an annual personal budget set by decision of the General Assembly of the kibbutz each year on an egalitarian basis.

Kibbutzim began primarily as agricultural settlements and only at a later stage entered into large-scale industrialization and other economic activities ranging from tourism to legal offices. In the early 1990's, agriculture continued to be an important factor in the kibbutz economy, and contributed more than one-third of the country's total agricultural produce; but industry had meanwhile expanded rapidly and came to contribute a larger direct share of gross kibbutz income. From another point of view, though, agriculture has remained dominant, since food-processing and manufacture of agricultural equipment account for more than half of total kibbutz industrial sales.

By 1991, kibbutz industry accounted for 7% of Israel's total industrial sales, and for 9% of its industrial exports (excluding diamonds). These figures become more meaningful when placed against the weight of the kibbutz, which in 1991 was only 2.6% of total Israeli population.

The above figures are one indication of the efficiency and high productivity that characterize the kibbutz economy. They lead inevitably to the question of whether the socioeconomic system of the kibbutz could be copied in a different social, economic, political, and cultural context. The question is particularly relevant for those countries where improved levels of productivity in agriculture and industry are urgently needed, and at the same time cultural tradition facilitates the adoption of communal consumption. Experience has taught that success in a kibbutz requires a high degree of personal commitment on the part of its membership to the communal way of life. That means developing an ideology capable of creating that measure of personal commitment to a vision until achievement of concrete results is able to produce its own justification.

Historically, the kibbutz developed as a part of Zionism, which provided strong ideological support for the commitment of members who saw in the kibbutz an efficient means for achieving the Zionist goal of regrouping the Jewish people in their traditional homeland. Another contributing factor was strong motivation for building a new and better way of life in the communitarian tradition, something which has been cultivated with much idealistic intensity in the youth movements. Any attempt to build kibbutzim elsewhere would require a comparable ideological motivation of high intensity.

The kibbutz movement is a revolutionary movement that carries several important socioeconomic messages for the 21st century. In an important sense, it is also a kind of "laboratory" for testing alternative socioeconomic practices. One important lesson from kibbutz experience is that labor, when liberated from market conditions by turning the worker into a participant-owner, becomes more meaningful and humane. It is also more efficient and reaches higher levels of productivity. Another important lesson is that flexible communal consumption, which allows for private needs and personal choice, is a better way of coping with the culture of consumerism cultivated by the expanding world market.

Altogether, the kibbutz has emerged as a new household model based on a community of families and comrades, who combine their skills and strengths in order to build a qualitatively and morally better way of life. It contrasts with contemporary market society in important ways: (1) the kibbutz encourages family members to stay together throughout the life-cycle, in contrast to private households where the elderly are usually left to fend for themselves and the young fail to derive adequate benefit from the experience of their parents; (2) kibbutz life is centered on people who are real and immediate, and not on abstractions such as prices and symbols of achievement; (3) the kibbutz is based on sharing and mutual help, and not on competition or the dominance of self-interest. In short, the kibbutz is based on the traditional values of the home and its distributive economy, and offers an alternative to the conflict of interests and resulting injustice which mark the exchange economy of contemporary local and international markets.

For a time, an impression was formed on the part of some members within, and some observers without, as though the family had only a minor role in the kibbutz. Actually, the kibbutz of today is one of the most "familial" societies in the world, and one of the few places where families of three and four generations continue to live together in the same household. Much attention is given in this monograph to the place of the family, partly because it is so important in itself and partly in order to set the record straight. That is one axis of the discussion. The other is concerned with the kibbutz as a shared household.

The past generation has seen the dynamic emergence of household economics as a respected field of inquiry, pulling together economists and a wide range of social scientists in what is developing as a new orientation of socioeconomics. The rise of consumerism as a dominant cultural trait of the expanding world market economy has given added importance to the household budget, with all its consequences. A significant change has come about with the understanding that households and families are not necessarily congruent. More and more households are being formed in post-industrial societies by domestic groups that are not families in the traditional sense of kinship.

Part of the new development has been a theory convenient for an exchange economy and according to which individuals build their lives on rational choices. That theory does not conform to one of the most important features of the emerging world market, which is the fact that billions of dollars are spent each year on advertising and other means of arousing demand for specific products, with the deliberate objective of producing irrational choices among consumers. In more affluent societies, professional marketing is devoted to creating wants were there are no existential needs.

Professional marketing experts have found that the shortest path to irrational choice is the cultivation of personal choice and individual consumption responding to real or presumed psychological needs. At the same time, there has been a persistent and unrelenting move in the other direction toward greater collective consumption in accordance with genuine social needs. Public services such as education, hospitals, police and fire departments, public parks and gardens, public transportation and the important communal care of the needy through unemployment compensation, old age pensions, municipal social welfare departments, etc., are only a part of the picture. All of them represent shared use of public facilities and resources.

In addition, there is the intriguing phenomenon of increasing demand for participation in mass events where the experience shared with many other persons is a vital element in attaining enjoyment, or some kind of satisfaction, from the event. In itself, participation in crowds is not a new phenomenon. Large-scale attendance at athletic events or religious festivals has been an important part of social activities in virtually all cultures of the world, and has for the most part demonstrated group solidarity along recognized and institutionalized lines. The now legendary musical festival at Woodstock, however, marked a profound and important change in two significant ways. First of all, the size of the crowd and the duration of the event were without precedent in advanced market societies. Secondly, identification with the music and its message indicated massive psychological needs that have not yet been defined fully, but are influencing social behavior. It is not accidental that the "rock" music associated with Woodstock, with its deep message of protest, has caught on in all parts of the world where rapid urbanization and faltering economic development, political incompetency, and the lingering menace of mass destruction from non-conventional weapons, have made anxiety a universal cultural trait.

Public response has not been restricted to music. There has been an extraordinary increase in the number of persons participating in political demonstrations and environmental protests. Then too, there is the relatively new phenomenon of mass participation in events filmed and shown simultaneously on television screens throughout the world in what are termed "live" programs, where viewers in the hundreds of millions share the same experience at the same time, and thereby also form a new kind of shared identity. The Olympic Games at Barcelona provided an unusually clear example of the new world culture based on participation of persons from all continents performing their roles according to an agreed set of rules, and brought into homes everywhere by a world communications network. The basic functional similarity between the Olympic Games and the emerging world market system is too clear to need further comment.

Whatever explanations may be offered, the fact of the matter is that there are two kinds of consumerism competing within the contemporary market culture, and they point in different directions. One moves toward greater individuation and personal choice, more privacy, and larger personal space. That trend is accompanied by weakening of the family group and its traditional pattern of shared living. The other trend is toward greater participation in group activities, more shared consumption, satisfaction of an inherent need for communication with other human beings, and strengthened self-identity through involvement in shared life with others. Together, they are creating a new world culture characterized by internal contradictions on a massive scale between rational and irrational choices.

The kibbutz is very much a part of that new world culture, and suffers from the same internal contradictions. Much of the recent "crisis" has been concerned with problems arising out of contradictions inherent in the attempts to meet rational and irrational choices within a common framework of shared consumption. Most of the criticism expressed in recent years has been aimed at failures in the functioning of the kibbutz household, and has been concerned with issues of consumerism. Greater demand for personal choices, and particularly those that are irrational, has made the allocation of household resources more difficult at a time when financial problems have compelled a reduction in the resources available for consumption.

The way in which the kibbutz copes with this problem, and the solutions it works out for combining greater individual consumption within a more flexible framework of shared consumption, are issues of immense importance for the future course of the emerging world market and its accompanying culture of consumerism. While the kibbutz grew out of specific historical conditions in the past, it is now an alternative way of life that is in the forefront of contemporary socioeconomic development. So far, it has had remarkable success in resolving problems through creative responses within concrete situations, but there have also been failures along the way and many mistakes made. This monograph is a modest attempt to bring some of the lessons from kibbutz experience to a wider public.

The present kibbutz population is divided into four organizational groups, each of which considers itself an independent movement within the overall framework commonly referred to as the "kibbutz movement". Largest among the four is the United Kibbutz Movement, usually called TAKAM according to its Hebrew acronym. It includes 61% of total kibbutz population in 166 kibbutzim. Next in size is the Kibbutz Artzi, with 32% of total kibbutz population in 85 kibbutzim. Much smaller are the two religious groups; the Kibbutz Dati with 6% of total kibbutz population in 17 kibbutzim, and Poeley Agudat Israel with 1% of total kibbutz population in 2 kibbutzim.

Kibbutz Maayan Zvi, November 1992

Chapter One
BACKGROUND

Beginnings of the kibbutz are to be found in the dramatic story of young Jewish men and women who became the pioneering builders of modern Israel. Most of them came from eastern Europe, and they began reaching what was then Palestine in the latter part of the 19th century. They came out of a social background still strongly rooted in rabbinic traditions of law and heavily saturated with Hasidic strains of mysticism. Almost all of the young pioneers had broken with tradition, identified with the dominant secular culture of Europe, and responded to persistent and often violent anti-semitism by adopting an ideological synthesis composed of nationalism along modern European lines, socialism heavily influenced by Russian revolutionary ideas skewed according to Biblical teachings of social justice, and a mystical acceptance of Biblical passages confirming historical rights to the ancient homeland of the Hebrews. Formation of the Zionist Organization facilitated translation of that ideology into practical measures and accelerated the pace of immigration and settlement. Replacement of Turkish rule in Palestine by the British Mandate after World War I permitted more efficiently organized activity, even when British policy opposed expansion of Jewish settlement.

Thousands of young men and women arrived with the intention of dedicating themselves to building the foundation for revived Hebrew national life. Those young men and women understood that they must take upon themselves the task of building the material foundations virtually with their bare hands since the economic infrastructure of the country was at a primitive level, and the Zionist Organization did not have the funds needed for a significant development program. The young pioneers became manual laborers and worked wherever needed, doing hard physical work at a subsistence wage level. In order to survive, they banded together in communes that·served them as substitutes for the homes and families they had left behind. That communal arrangement allowed them to survive in the difficult conditions of the time, even with only a minimal income.

The communes were formed as small shared households, usually with fewer than a dozen members. Those who were lucky enough to find work, put their pay into a common treasury which supported all members of the commune. According to reports of the time, frequently only a few were able to find work while perhaps an equal number were sick, and the remaining members cooked and took care of them.

In the year 1910, one of the communes was offered a tract of land that had earlier been purchased by the Zionist Organization. It was located alongside the Jordan River and close to the southern shores of Lake Kinneret (Sea of Galilee). Members of the commune agreed to accept the land on the condition that they would also be responsible for management of the farm operations. They called their new agricultural settlement Degania, and it became the first of the kibbutzim as they are now known. The original group was made up of a dozen young men and women, all of them single with no children. Since then, hundreds of other kibbutzim have been formed following the same basic pattern of an initial core group of young singles that expands through absorption of new members, and then grows chiefly through increase in the children's population, eventually followed by acceptance into membership of kibbutz sons and daughters along with their marriage partners (who are usually not from the same kibbutz).

In the past, most of the core groups were formed in Zionist youth movements, which enjoyed widespread popularity between the two World Wars. The largest of them were in Poland and central Europe, but they were almost entirely wiped out during the Holocaust. That catastrophe had a crippling effect on continued growth of the kibbutz movement. Extinction of the large Zionist youth movements in eastern and central Europe reduced the stream of new core groups from abroad to a mere trickle, and led to a sharp reduction in the number of new kibbutzim established. Most kibbutzim formed since the Holocaust have been based on core groups from within Israel or from North and South America.

Historical Periods

Defining historical periods is always a controversial issue since it depends to a large extent on evaluation of events according to their presumed importance, and that is often determined by subjective interpretation or ideology rather than by the facts. The following schema has the same weakness, but seems to the author to be at least useful in ordering the facts.

The first period, covering the quarter of a century from 1910 to 1935, was characterized by experimentation, adaptation to hard facts of life, much theoretical discussion about what a kibbutz ought to be, a good deal of mobility into and out of kibbutzim, and even mobility of kibbutzim from one organizational-ideological framework to another. In short, it was a formative period with emphasis more on vision than on reality. Both economically and socially, there were more failures than successes. Many observers, including professional economists and social scientists, were convinced that the kibbutz couldn't prove self-supporting and self-perpetuating. Only minimal financial support was given by the Zionist financial institutions, and the total result was that the kibbutzim suffered from inadequate means of production and a persistently low standard of living. Most of the hard-core members responded to the difficult cirumstances by making poverty their hallmark, with bare feet and tattered clothes as their signs of identification. Understandably in such circumstances, many of those who entered kibbutzim viewed their experience as only temporary, and almost all of the kibbutzim suffered from prolonged instability.

The second period began in 1936, when the Arab population of Palestine rose up in rebellion against the British Mandate authority. At the same time, there were high-level discussions about partition into two separate states, one Jewish and one Arab. A third element was the large number of refugees arriving from Germany. The Zionist leadership recognized that the situation required rapid expansion of Jewish settlements in order to influence favorably the future choice of borders for a Jewish state; to provide increased security in the hinterlands for existing settlements; and to provide additional locations where legal and illegal Jewish immigrants could be received, housed, fed and provided with work outside of the already overcrowded cities. Political and security considerations now became more important than those of economic viability. Clearly, kibbutzim were the most expedient way of settling remote areas quickly and cheaply, and of assuring safe and flexible arrangements for the reception of new immigrants. Kibbutz members were willing to endure hardships and confront dangers more than most of the civilian population, which preferred the comforts and security of urban life.

Funds were now found for the establishment of many new kibbutzim, from the northern borders with Lebanon and Syria down to the heart of the Negev. An intensive program for covering the land with kibbutzim continued until shortly after formation of the State of Israel. By that time, almost half of all Jewish settlements were kibbutzim. Eventually, they played a vital role in the war against the Arabs and in determining the borders that were ultimately accepted in the cease-fire agreements of 1949. That story is one of the most dramatic and important chapters in the history of the kibbutz, but does not belong to the present account.

The third period began in 1950. With establishment of the State of Israel, the gates were opened for unhampered immigration, and masses of Jews poured into the country. Priorities changed. The kibbutz model, overwhelmingly secular and attuned to ideas familar in European culture, was judged by high officials to be unsuitable for most of the new immigrants coming from North African and Asian communities. Preference in absorbing those immigrants was given to the moshav model of cooperative family farming, and soon hundreds of additional moshavim were set up, while support for the kibbutzim dwindled.

Kibbutz members made a painful adjustment to their new status as just plain citizens and no longer as central partners in execution of Zionist policy. There was difficulty in making an ideological adjustment to the administrative framework imposed by the State as the kibbutz had been nourished in no small measure from anarchistic sources. Participation in party politics soon degenerated from high-level policy commitments to power confrontations as the kibbutz movement used its superior organization to gain tactical advantages and relatively high representation in government office. Many members were disappointed with the change and left their kibbutz with the feeling that it had served its purpose and had no further justification for existence. Others, who remained, saw no need to perpetuate the conditions of poverty, particularly in view of the rapid rise in standard of living experienced in the surrounding society. Major attention was turned to developing a permanent life-style and ensuring economic success. Better housing was constructed, more emphasis was placed on a stable and comfortable way of life.

The first large groups of kibbutz youths from the second generation came of age and became members. They looked to the future more than to the past, rejected some of the old ideological positions that had been attuned to a different reality, insisted on higher education, and no longer saw manual labor as a value in itself. They soon acquired a relatively high degree of technological and professional competency, assumed key positions in the kibbutz economy, promoted widespread application of new methods of production, and soon brought kibbutz agriculture to the forefront on a worldwide scale. They also initiated significant expansion of kibbutz industry. However, they showed relatively little interest in national politics and contented themselves with involvement in local or regional affairs. Many members no longer saw kibbutz life as a goal of value in itself comparable in importance to pursuing an academic or administrative career, and left to find their place in the surrounding society. For the same reasons, fewer joined kibbutzim from the youth movements and from the cities. One of the low points came in 1961, when there was a drop of one thousand persons in net population.

That period ended with the Six-Day War. Kibbutz members played a prominent role in the military success and once again proved the importance of kibbutzim from the security point of view. After the war, the Israeli government supported accelerated industrialization of the country, and offered financial support on generous terms. The kibbutz movement, which had already been moving in that direction, now saw an opportunity for a rapid breakthrough which would contribute to achieving an important national goal, would provide a wider range of job opportunities for members, and would create badly needed additional sources of income.

The fourth period, from 1967 to 1992, was dominated by rapid and widespread industrialization that changed the kibbutz from an agricultural community into a new kind of socioeconomic formation, which has yet to be clearly defined. Hundreds of factories were built in kibbutzim, beginning in areas closest to agriculture: food processing and agricultural equipment. Production of plastic products proved particularly suitable to kibbutz conditions, and soon one half of the entire Israeli plastics industry was located in kibbutzim. By 1991, total industrial sales reached two billion dollars, of which one third were for export. Productivity of workers was consistently higher than in non-kibbutz industries.

Economic success attracted a lot of new members during the 1970's and early 1980's, particularly young families who had become disappointed with urban life and recognized the advantages for themselves and their children in the kibbutz way of life. The demographic stagnation which characterized the third period came to an end, and was followed in the fourth period by an process of rapid growth. Between 1967 and 1987, kibbutz population grew by 53%, from 83,100 to 127,000.

Meanwhile, Israel was going through a dismally ill-conceived and mismanaged attempt under Likud dominated governments (headed by Menahem Begin and Yitzhak Shamir) to move from a mixed to a free market economy. The result was soaring inflation that reached 400% annually, followed by a sudden braking of the economy through a freeze on prices and wages, and then an extended period of high interest rates intended to keep the economy cooled down with low inflation. In the productive sectors, input costs rose faster than income and thousands of firms went into bankruptcy, while the stock market enjoyed some of the best years in its history. Since the kibbutz economy is concentrated almost entirely in agriculture and industry, it had great vulnerability and experienced large losses, but no kibbutz took refuge in bankruptcy and no kibbutz collapsed under the growing debt load. Within just a few years, the cumulative debt load of the entire kibbutz movement tripled and approached four billion dollars at a time when total gross income from all sources came to just over three and a half billion dollars.

There were several contributing factors in producing such a large debt load. One was the poor performance of the Israeli economy, which severely reduced profitability in agriculture and industry. A second was the extensive investments made by kibbutzim in industry and in housing in order to cope with the rapid growth in population by providing more jobs and housing, and that at a time when there was no comparable growth in net income. A third explanation is managerial inadequacy as a direct result of the kibbutz economy growing faster in size and complexity than the comparable growth in available managerial skills. It should be recalled that it has been customary for managers to come from within the kibbutz population, not from the surrounding labor market, and most prior experience of kibbutz managers had been primarily in agriculture.

Errors of judgment were made in handling financial matters, and that contributed to an atmosphere of increasing insecurity within kibbutzim. A wave of departures followed on a scale not known for many years, while fewer people applied for admission. Of serious social consequence was the relatively high concentration of young people leaving, and especially young families who left with their children. One immediate result was a sharp fall in the number of births and a decline in the children's population of pre-school age.

According to data published by the Israeli Central Bureau of Statistics, there was a net decline in kibbutz population in the years 1988 and 1989, for the first time in more than twenty years. Questions were once again raised about the viability of the kibbutz, and particularly its ability to survive in a world dominated by a market economy. Soon the financial crisis of the kibbutz drew worldwide attention, became the subject of a number of doctoral dissertations, and brought many "experts" to conclude that the kibbutz was about to go the way of other revolutionary experiments. What many have failed to realize is that the entire history of the kibbutz has been an unending saga of crises, with that of the late 1980's not the most serious or threatening when compared with earlier ones, and certainly not when judged in concrete terms of demographic changes.

Despite the financial difficulties, and particularly the shortage of capital for purchase of raw materials even when firm orders were in hand, the kibbutz economy was been able to continue functioning and even in some cases to expand. Some inefficient plants were closed. Richer kibbutzim helped poorer ones, new sources of income were developed, and measures were taken for much stricter managerial supervision. Even the more troubled kibbutzim stood firm, and no established kibbutz collapsed, though a dozen new settlements had to be abandoned because the movement could not afford the expense of populating them and developing in them a viable economy. On the other hand, many of those who earlier left their kibbutz because of the uncertain future have returned after becoming convinced that the kibbutz way of life is preferable to living elsewhere. Meanwhile, a temporary restructuring of the debt has been arranged with the banks and the government, in the largest economic operation carried out in Israel's history, but there remains awareness on the part of all concerned that a more permanent arrangement has yet to be worked out.

What recent experience has proved is that (1) on the operational side, the kibbutz must do more to improve the quality of its management; (2) on the policy side, it still has to produce a feasible way of integrating its unique distributive economy into the exchange economy of the expanding world market, and (3) the kibbutz community has reached a point of social development where it is strong enough to withstand severe crises without danger to its continued existence.

The year 1989 was the low point. An upturn began in 1990, and then in 1991 there was a significant improvement with a record population growth rate of 3.4%, and an increase of 4.7% in industrial sales. The major source of population growth was massive absorption of immigrants coming from the former Soviet Union, while the main improvement in industrial sales came from the expanded domestic market. There has also been an increase in the number of young people from the kibbutz who have chosen to remain, or who have returned after having previously left their kibbutz.

The following table summarizes population changes for the period of 1985-1991 according to data published by the Government of Israel's Central Bureau of Statistics.

CHANGES IN KIBBUTZ POPULATION 1985-1991

Year	Natural Reproduction	Migration Balance	Net Growth	End of Year
1985	2,300	200	2,500	125,200
1986	2,200	- 700	1,500	126,700
1987	1,900	- 1,600	300	127,000
1988	1,700	- 2,600	- 900	126,100
1989	1,500	- 2,700	- 1,200	124,900
1990	1,500	- 1,300	200	125,100
1991	1,300	2,900	4,200	129,300

Chapter Two
SOCIAL DEVELOPMENT

Zionist youth movements in Israel and abroad are based on an ideological commitment to rebuilding Jewish national life in Israel. For many years the largest of them were connected to the kibbutz movement and prepared their members for the highest form of Zionist self-actualization, which was commonly agreed to be found in kibbutz life. That was during the heroic period of pioneering and widespread establishment of new settlements under difficult conditions that called for a high degree of self-sacrifice. After creation of the State of Israel and the accompanying changes in the status of the kibbutz, the message received in the youth movements also changed, and so did the priorities of the young people, but that is getting ahead of the story. This chapter is concerned with how most of the existing kibbutzim got started, their typical process of growth, and the lessons that can be learned from past experience for the future.

Along with the strong shared Zionist commitment that unified groups within those youth movements ideologically, there was also a process of socialization that proved no less important in building group solidarity. Such groups were trained to become founders of new kibbutzim or support for existing kibbutzim. They are called nuclear or "seed" groups because they are intended to be the start of an expanding formation. These nuclear groups are formed in the youth movements by young men and women in their adolescence. Their members pass through intense shared experiences as they go through a process of socialization, formation of group identity, preparatory training of one kind or another, and then the actual work of building a new kibbutz or reinforcing an older one -- and all of this during the most sensitive years of their lives. In addition, the shared passage from adolescence to manhood or womanhood while living and working together creates an intimate feeling of solidarity which contributes much to making the initial group into a genuine community of comrades. The bonds created between them usually remain strong and meaningful until the end of their lives. Nuclear groups of that kind founded most existing kibbutzim.

Once a new kibbutz is started, the first decade (and sometimes into the second as well) is a decisive period of transition from a mobile community of comrades, that have come from elsewhere, to a stable and rooted primary group prepared to carry the responsibilities of permanent communal life. Some members of the nuclear group are not able to make the adjustment and choose to leave. Much attention is paid to absorbing new members in order to grow as quickly as possible. The newcomers may be groups or individuals. There is a period of relatively high social mobility as some leave and others join, and as a result of these changes initial social solidarity weakens. Newer members cannot become an integral part of the older group and its intense inner solidarity as formed by the older members, for they were not participants in the shared experiences that formed the primary group. At the same time, the first children are born, and their parents are anxious to accelerate progress toward a more stable environment with properly functioning services.

Maturation as a Social Process

The intensely personal and unified community of the founding members gives way to plurality and compromise as the kibbutz grows in size, expands and becomes a continually more diversified social body. In order to hold the kibbutz together and ensure satisfactory functioning in daily life, it becomes more and more necessary to clarify common objectives and the principles governing the kibbutz way of life. Where the close personal bonds between the founding members held the initial community together and guided the decision-making process, now the shared ideological framework becomes more important in holding the more diversified community together as the decision-making process becomes more institutionalized.

During the initial stage, almost all of the founding members are single, and that adds to the solidarity of the fledgling kibbutz as a personal community. It does not take long, however, for families to be formed. The transition from primary identification with the age group to a proliferation of binary relations with marriage partners, further weakens the initial unity. As children are born and the discrete family units become increasingly more important in the social life of the members, some become concerned about the consequences of this trend and its implications for the future. They fear the disruptive influence that the emerging nuclear family may have on communal solidarity.

In the past, measures were frequently taken to restrain the emergence of "familialism" because of its divisive tendencies toward private relations and feelings of private possession. Another reason for opposition to familialism was the belief that the liberation of women could be achieved only by destroying the economic power of the nuclear family. In the societies of eastern and central Europe from which most of the early kibbutz members had come, that power gave to the male head of the small family control over his wife and children almost as though they were his private property. Women spent much of their time engaged in routine household chores, accepting sevice to their husbands and children as their main purpose in life. The idea was to eliminate that bondage by ensuring that all economic power was in the hands of the entire community, with the women as equal members.

In order to ensure primacy of the community, all means of production and all income from whatever source were placed under communal control. Consumption was also made communal with the communal dining hall as the very center of kibbutz life. Attempts to enlarge the separate sphere of the individual family into a distinct household (such as introducing even the rudiments of a separate kitchen) or enlarging the personal budget beyond immediate personal needs, were opposed in the past with varying degrees of intensity depending on the age, ideological formation, and general maturity of the contestants.

As the kibbutz grew and became more affluent, attempts were made to ensure adequate variety in communal consumption so as to meet individual desires and needs. Where this could not be done, personal budgets were expanded so that each member could acquire what he needed in accordance with his personal taste. The result has been a system of personal budgets that allows the individual member to purchase a wide variety of goods and services according to his own inclinations. That development has been a major concession to the consumer culture of the market society. At the time of writing these lines in 1992, communal consumption still accounts for the majority of household expenses, and apparently shall remain so, though the subject is under discussion in a number of kibbutzim. Kibbutz members do not receive any wages or direct remuneration for their work since one of the objectives has been to remove work from the labor market. Strong resistance to increased personal budgets comes from those who do not want an opening for implementation of any kind of monetary or other "payment" in exchange for work performed. On the other hand, personal budgets do allow much more flexibility in coping with the consumer culture that is becoming ever more dominant in Israel, as elsewhere in the world.

Inevitably, the move toward personal budgets has given rise to fears that the combined and strengthed trends of familialism and consumerism must eventually lead to a break-up of the communal household into diverse nuclear family households, private accounts, and competition for higher incomes and more possessions. Separate and differential incomes would mean formation of individual households and an end to the communal household. The financial problems of the late 1980's stimulated pressures in that direction, but when the subject was brought to the representative bodies of TAKAM and Kibbutz Artzi for a policy decision, linkage between work and remuneration was rejected by an overwhelming majority.

Sources of Communal Solidarity

Because many kibbutz members in the earlier stages saw in the family, as a discrete social unit, a threat to continued solidarity of the kibbutz, efforts were made to restrain familial impulses. Although couples had "family rooms", they were expected to restrict their personal relations to the privacy of that room. Men and women regarded one another as comrades in building a new way of life, and such terms as "husband" and "wife" were rejected as belonging to the society they had left behind. Each was supposed to have his own individual life within the community, according to the highest ideals of woman's emancipation.

Children were grouped together in separate children's houses for purposes of security as well as to attain maximum freedom for the mothers, and also (some would say primarily) because that system allowed better living conditions for the children than were available in the tents and wooden huts that were then the prevalent housing of their parents. Education within the children's houses was based on the principle of socialization within a peer group. Members of the peer groups, who lived and grew up together, formed very close relations and often felt more attached to one another than to their siblings. In more recent years, most of the kibbutzim have changed the system and now have the children sleeping in their parents' apartment. Peer groups have tended to give way to age groups, and yet the bonds formed during childhood within a shared household contine to provide an important source of solidarity within the community as the young people mature and become active members.

In the beginning, work within the kibbutz was based on direct participation of each member in some group which functioned as a team. Each team had responsibility for some part of the production and service operations within the overall kibbutz framework. Management was conducted collectively, with each member of the team able to participate in the decision-making. In agriculture and the services, the head of the team has traditionally been called "organizer" in the egalitarian sense of coordinator, and not manager. This system still prevails in most branches of agriculture and the services, but there has been difficulty in maintaining a similar structure within the context of industrialization and formation of factories with relatively large numbers of workers. A partial solution has been found by organizing the work as much as possible on the basis of teams. Nevertheless, a generally hierarchical structure of the work force has become widespread in kibbutz industry, particularly in the larger plants, and in most if not all cases the head of the factory or other enterprise is called manager.

The experience of close and continuing inter-relationship with other members of the team on a day-to-day basis creates strong personal bonds which have proven to be another important source of social solidarity, though over the long run they can also be a source of friction and tension. Experience teaches that successful communal living also requires the option of social distance. As the kibbutz grows from the initial personal community to a large social grouping of several hundred members, the very size of the kibbutz as well as the diversity in age and temperament of the members creates the social distance needed while maintaining the advantages of a shared household. However, the movement from homogeneous personal community to heterogeneous social community has often been identified with the process of institutionalization that has characterized the development of modern market societies. Social development in the kibbutz is different because it is based on integration of the two, rather than counterposing them as conflicting alternatives.

While the social community grows in size and diversity, there are countervailing forces at work which strengthen areas of personal solidarity. The peer group of those born and raised together is one. The work-team is another. Participation in decision-making, whether in committees or in the general assembly, is still another. Surprisingly, though, the most important source of personal solidarity has turned out to be the family! What many had not foreseen is that broad transfer of economic control to the kibbutz, and the practice of communal consumption, would turn the kibbutz into a communal household capable of absorbing all the children who wish to remain as members, thereby making possible the formation of multi-generation families living within the same shared home. The result has been the social formation of a strong familial community within the framework of a technologically advanced economy. Release of the family as a human group from economic bonds has strengthened the personal relations and encouraged younger people to remain with their parents in a situation where there are no relations of economic dependency or control between them.

A summary description of development within a kibbutz would take into account the progression from a founding group of young people, through the stages of their maturation and formation of families, and ultimately to creation of a community based on large family units of three and even four generations. In contemporary urban market societies, each nuclear family is a separate economic unit, with control of the purse in the hands of the parents. Inevitably, economic relations and love relations become confused, economic and emotional dependency conflict, and the use of economic pressure on the part of parents proves harmful to the healthy development of personal bonds between the generations. An important lesson from kibbutz experience is that such an economic arrangement does more to divide families than to unite them. Egoistic economic interests are not compatible with a pattern of loving personal relations motivated by altruism. The process of mixing them in the market society has brought the inevitable result of weakening the family as the market culture favors egoism over altruism. In contrast, the kibbutz family is characterized by a continual process of growth and expansion. The extraordinary personal solidarity that develops within the extended kibbutz family is a major contribution to the strength of the social fabric. Possible tendencies toward familial separatism or formation of discrete "interest groups" are attenuated by the balancing solidarity created within peer groups, work teams, or other social formations within which each member of a family participates.

The familial community within the kibbutz grows slowly, like an organic body, and no kibbutz can be called mature until it has reached its third generation. It is not an organization, where members can come and go while the fundamental structure of the organization remains unchanged. The kibbutz community is a living body, and for continued health there must be proper internal balance between the parts, as well as a continued infusion of new life through the addition of new members who can be absorbed and find their place as responsible adults within the community, whether they come from within or are absorbed from without.

Chapter Three
MOBILITY AND CONTINUITY

Every kibbutz grows out of a mobile population which originally comes from somewhere else. The decisive period in formation of the permanent settlement is when a part of the population becomes rooted in the place and forms a stable familial foundation upon which the community then grows. In the process, this core group pushes the more mobile or transient elements to the periphery, and the kibbutz assumes its permanent character as a familial community which is also strongly influenced by the earlier tradition and retains many of the traits of comradeship.

Thousands of communes have been formed throughout the world in the past, and almost all of them turned out to be only temporary phenomena because they insisted on preserving the personal freedom of social mobility. That is to say, they allowed members to come and go as they pleased.[1] Kibbutz experience shows that absolute personal freedom of movement is harmful to the community's continuity and must be limited by strong commitment to the community and its future. Since the contemporary market society stresses the importance of personal mobility on a world-wide scale, and the kibbutz requires rootedness and continuity, a conflict between the two frequently becomes inevitable, and particularly among the young.

From Mobility to Continuity

The social formation in all established kibbutzim is that of a core population made up of permanent members and their children, an intermediary stable population of parents and other residents who live in the kibbutz for relatively long periods, and around them a mobile periphery of more or less transient or temporary residents. During the earlier years,

---

[1] The literature is vast, but for recent developments it is sufficient to study the broad range of data provided by Benjamin Zablocki, ALIENATION AND CHARISMA, The Free Press, New York, 1980. A comprehensive study of past communal experiments in America can be found in Yaacov Oved's, TWO HUNDRED YEARS OF AMERICAN COMMUNES, Transaction Publishers, New Brunswick, 1988.

the difference between the three is not very apparent since most of the population is made up of young people of the same age group, working together and sharing very simple living conditions, and all of whom have come from some other place only a short while before.

Social "take-off" in growth of a kibbutz takes place with emergence of a strong familial foundation that enlarges and stabilizes the core group, making it clearly dominant, while the temporary population becomes marginal. In established contemporary kibbutzim the core population is between 80-90% of the total population. The period required to achieve social "take-off" with a firm familial foundation has varied considerably through the years. In early kibbutzim it sometimes took as long as two decades. Most of the more recently established kibbutzim have been able to achieve it within the first decade.

Founding members of early kibbutzim, as well as outside observers, frequently complained about the restlessness of young people from eastern Europe following the First World War and the Russian Revolution. Many of those young people came to kibbutz life inspired by the revolutionary ideal of radical change in socioeconomic conditions, but routine physical labor under trying circumstances quickly diminished their enthusiasm, with the result that sooner or later they left for less demanding challenges. Others came only to gain work experience in one or another of the branches existing in kibbutzim, and then left to seek their fortune as hired laborers in the private sector or to set up their own farm.

According to a census of 20 kibbutzim taken in 1930, their total population was 2,143. Of that number, 1,887 or 88% made up the core group (comprising 523 children, 777 male adults, and 587 female adults), while the rest were dependent relatives or temporaries and their children. A further analysis reveals that a quarter of the men and women had been in their kibbutz less than two years. Of the total population, most of the children were between the ages of 0-5, while most of the adults were between 21-30. Half of the men and 70% of the women were married, forming 438 families of which the majority had no more than one child.

In another census taken in the same year among 24 kibbutzim, there was a total population of 2,566 made up of 624 children and 1,942 adults aged 17 and over. Of the adults, 55% were married. They made up 505 families with two parents and 53 one-parent families. A quarter of the families were without children, 45% had one child, and another quarter had two children. Three-quarters of the children were between the ages of 0-5. Of the adults, most were between the ages of 21-30.

Waves of immigrants coming in from Europe in the 1930's, and among them many refugees from Nazi Germany, contributed to rapid growth in kibbutz population and continuation of the high proportion of newcomers. The frequent movement of population, with relatively large groups entering and leaving often gave members the feeling that their kibbutz was more "like a train station". Nevertheless, a familial foundation formed in each kibbutz and the core group strengthened. Not all of the kibbutzim were in the same situation. In the older kibbutzim, the core adult population grew slowly while the childrens' population grew rapidly. Most of the adult newcomers were absorbed in new kibbutzim that were set up at a rapid pace.

As can be seen in the following table, almost one-third of the kibbutz population in 1948 had been in the country for less than four years. Among the adults the proportion was even higher since most of the new immigrants were adults, while most of the Israel-born were children.

KIBBUTZ POPULATION IN 1948

Year of Immigration	Male	Female	Total	Percentages
Up to 1919	114	70	184	0.3
1919-1932	2,292	2,095	4,387	8.1
1933-1936	3,428	3,401	6,829	12.6
1937-1940	3,205	2,435	5,640	10.4
1941-1944	1,361	803	2,164	4.0
1945-1948	9,448	7,385	16,833	31.1
Unknown	108	104	212	0.4
Born in Israel	9,366	8,593	17,959	33.1
Total	29,322	24,886	54,208	100.0

Source: Population Census of 1948, Central Bureau of Statistics, Govt. of Israel.

Since most of the new immigrants were young adults, they contributed to maintaining a low average age level in the kibbutz population as a whole. At the time of the census, children aged 0-4 made up 15% of the kibbutz population and age group 15-29 made up another 40%.

AGE STRUCTURE IN 1948

	Male	Female	Total	Percentages
0 - 4	4,241	3,921	8,162	15.1
5 - 9	2,343	2,212	4,555	8.4
10 - 14	2,093	1,790	3,883	7.2
15 - 19	4,462	3,747	8,209	15.1
20 - 24	4,343	3,407	7,750	14.3
25 - 29	3,532	2,403	5,935	10.9
30 - 34	2,775	2,536	5,311	9.8
35 - 39	2,862	2,485	5,347	9.9
40 - 44	1,300	966	2,266	4.2
45 - 49	584	448	1,032	1.9
50 +	719	913	1,632	3.0
Unknown	68	58	126	0.2
Total	29,322	24,886	54,208	100.0

Source: Population Census of 1948, Central Bureau of Statistics, Govt. of Israel.

In older kibbutzim, living conditions had been difficult and the pervading uncertainty about the future impeded development of a stable and permanent population during the first two or three decades. With establishment of the State of Israel circumstances changed. Income rose, and soon there was better housing and other facilities. The second generation came of age and contributed significantly to more technologically advanced production. At the same time, the number of newcomers dropped considerably and the core population was able to assure its dominance over the transient elements. Younger kibbutzim made the transition much more rapidly.

For example, Kinneret began as a kibbutz alongside of Degania in 1913. By 1926 it had only 60 members and 15 children. Fourteen years later, in 1940, there were 172 members and 112 children. Of the 74 then existing families, 13 had no children, 31 had one child, 17 had two children, and 13 had three children or more. In addition, there was a peripheral population of 91 (24.3%). Fifty years later, Kinneret had a core population of 514 members and 221 children, and a peripheral population of only 52 (6.6%). In addition, 45% of the members were kibbutz-born, and Kinneret had become a strong familial community.

Another veteran kibbutz, Ayalet Hashahar located in the upper Galilee, was established during the First World War. After 12 years, there were 70 adults aged 16 or over, and most them were still single. Of the 16 then existing families, 2 had no children, 11 had one child, and 3 had 2 children. At the end of another ten years, in 1940, there were 204 members of whom only 39 were single. There were 84 families, of which 15 had no children, 44 had one child, 20 had two children, and 5 had three children or more. In addition, there was a peripheral population of 118 (27.4%), making for a total population of 431. Fifty years later, in 1990, Ayalet Hashahar had a core population of 565 members and 299 children, and a peripheral population of 95 (9.9%), making for a total population of 959. Half of the members were kibbutz-born, and that is the clearest indication of how strong the familial foundation has become.

The process moved at a faster pace in younger kibbutzim. The primary group of Sdot Yam was formed in 1935, and its settlement on the central coast was carried out in 1940. By 1946 there was a core population of 133 members and 44 children, plus a peripheral population of 40 (18%). Ten years later, in 1957, there were 225 members and 198 children. Of the members, only 39 had belonged to the primary group. An additional 84 had joined the kibbutz during the first decade after its establishment, and another 99 during the second decade (with data for three members unknown). There were 6 families with no children, 24 with one child, 62 with two children, 63 with three children, and 20 with four children. In 1970 there were 274 members, of whom 66 were kibbutz-born. In 1990, Sdot Yam had a core population of 409 members and 208 children, plus a peripheral population of 22 (3.4%). Of the members, 132 were kibbutz-born.

The primary group that founded Kibbutz Beeri in the Negev was made up of two parts, the first of which formed in 1942. The settlement was established in 1946. In 1957 there were 135 members and 95 children. Almost two-thirds of the members had joined after the second year of the settlement. There were already 8 families with no children, 20 families with one child, 28 families with two children, 25 families with three children, and 8 families with four children. In 1970, Beeri had 238 members, of whom 57 were kibbutz-born. Twenty years later, in 1990, Beeri had a core population of 462 members and 275 children, plus a peripheral population of 108 (12.8%). A third of the members were kibbutz-born.

The process of development from a primary group to a mature kibbutz is accompanied by a social change from a voluntary and therefore artificial grouping of young founding members, who initially came together for ideological and/or other reasons, to a natural community welded together by a shared way of life, comradeship and kinship. That change involves a transition from a society of contemporaries with little age differentiation to a natural community with a full age span. Most kibbutz families now include at least three generations, with most kibbutz children growing up alongside grandparents as a natural way of life, and in that way the young become aware from early age of what a full life cycle means.

The Continuity of Change

Kibbutzim in the 1960's had little resemblance to kibbutzim of the 1930's, either in physical appearance or in social constitution. Similarly, kibbutzim in the 1990's have little resemblance physically or socially to kibbutzim of the 1960's. Major population changes had taken place during the period of rapid growth in the 1970's and early 1980's. The heroic pioneering stage of the kibbutz, dominated by members who had been trained in the youth movements, had become past history. Members born and raised in the kibbutz, together with their marriage partners from elsewhere, had become the main part of the social fabric. Life in the kibbutz had moved from an operational to a permanent basis. The problems of everyday life took on more importance than abstract issues of ideology. For most, the kibbutz way of life had become an end in itself, and not a means for attaining national or other objectives. As such, the kibbutz had to justify itself in meeting the existential needs of its members, and that became difficult in many kibbutzim where the financial squeeze was most severe.

In the oldest kibbutz, veteran members who had been among the founders and early builders passed away and for their sons and grandsons the kibbutz had a different meaning. Of the many who immigrated to Israel during the first four waves of immigration (1881-1931) and contributed to building the early kibbutzim, only 3,752 were in kibbutzim in 1948. Their number was reduced to 1,710 by 1961, and in the early 1990's only a few old stalwarts remained. Meanwhile, significant demographic changes had taken place, with many young men and women accepted into membership.

According to the population census of 1961, 64% of total kibbutz population had been born elsewhere. Of them, half had been in their kibbutz less than ten years. According to a survey of some 82 kibbutzim belonging to Ihud Hakvuzot Ve–Hakibbutzim in 1974, during the decade of 1964-1973, 7,601 men and women had been accepted into membership or candidacy, and they represented 43% of the total. Of the newcomers, 45% were born and raised in the kibbutz, 6% were youths that had been educated in the kibbutz, 25% had come out of youth movements, and the remainder had no kibbutz or movement background. In 1991, 17,347 of the members and candidates of TAKAM had been accepted during the previous decade. Of them 47% had been born and raised in the kibbutz, 32% were Israelis without a movement background, 8% were from overseas without a movement background, 7% came from Israeli youth movements, 2% from overseas youth movements, and the remainder were youths who had been educated in a kibbutz.

The significant point is that while a traditional social structure has been developing in the kibbutz and ensuring continuity through the increasing share of kibbutz-born in the membership, at the same time the population has been changing relatively rapidly through two-way migration of members and candidates. Between 1960 and 1990, the number of kibbutz members grew rapidly. Most of the growth came from absorption of kibbutz-born youths and from persons with an urban background in Israel or abroad joining the kibbutz (in many cases as marriage partners of kibbutz members). A relatively small percentage of new members came from youth movements.

The often conflicting trends of continuity through expansion of the familial component and change through absorption of strangers have forced the kibbutz to maintain a dialectical balance between them in order to continue growing. In doing so, it is performing a unique experiment. On the one hand, the kibbutz has turned back to a firmly based traditional familial community within a clearly defined shared territory. On the other hand, the kibbutz is deeply immersed economically in the world market through relatively large-scale agricultural and industrial production for export, socially it is open and relatively mobile, and culturally it has adopted much of the consumerism prevailing in the surrounding market society. Experience shows that the combination is not easy. There is no stable balance between them, and conflict between the different trends is difficult to avoid. Moral strength is required to master the tension and remain balanced. Those who do not have the necessary moral strength soon find themselves out of balance and even out of the kibbutz by their own choosing.

The key to successful kibbutz development through the years is emergence of a traditional community based on kinship and lifetime comradeship between neighbors as the dominant trend. Out of this social process has come a way of life in which the individual finds himself within a pattern of human relations that stands in contrast to the dominant pattern of market relations prevalent elsewhere. Work is a part of life, and not a marketable product. At the same time, the kibbutz makes every effort to be in the forefront of technologically advanced agricultural and industrial production. It also strives to maintain a quality of life that utilizes constructively the best achievements of technologically advanced production of consumer products.

In contrast to many communal experiments of the past, the kibbutz from its beginnings has been involved socially, politically, and economically in the surrounding society. It has not been a flight from contemporary problems or from an evil world, but rather an attempt to find a better way to cope with reality. It is consciously and boldly an attempt to build a better socioeconomic system within the world and through involvement in the real problems confronting mankind. The challenge is enormous, the difficulties tremendous, and so far the achievements have been surprisingly positive.

Chapter Four
COMMUNITY IN A MARKET SOCIETY (I)

Soon, most of the world's population shall be concentrated in cities, both in the northern and southern hemispheres. Many persons, who view such developments with dismay and concern, turn nostalgically to the past and contrast contemporary urban society with former communal forms of social life. The very intensity of urbanization has spurred growth of communitarian trends based on pursuit of an alternative way of life. The kibbutz is a part of that movement, and has emerged in the twentieth century as the leading communitarian alternative to the problematic urban society of the expanding world market economy. The collective experience of the kibbutz has much to teach, both in what it has achieved and in what it has not been able to achieve.

The distinctive characteristic of the contemporary kibbutz, and that which separates it from most other communal experiments, is that it combines the advantages of an autonomous territorial base, a relatively large number of people living together as a community, a firm familial foundation that ensures commitment to continuity, and the socioeconomic structure of a single shared household. It is not a fragment of an urban complex, nor a voluntary social group of temporary duration, nor is it a village in the conventional sense. It is a single household serving the needs of an entire community, and its united strength is enough to insure long-term stability despite vagaries of the market.

Although given some consideration in the beginning, the idea of a self-sufficient or autarkic community was given up at an early stage, and instead the kibbutz pursued a policy of seeking integration in the surrounding economy through systems of cooperative marketing and purchasing that largely did away with the need for direct contact between individual kibbutz members and the surrounding market. That worked well as long as the kibbutz economy was primarily agricultural. However, when the kibbutz entered into a period of rapid industrialization it was not able to form a comparable system of cooperatives, and as a result almost every factory has had to assume direct responsibility for purchasing of raw materials and marketing of finished products in the world market. The net result has been closer integration of the kibbutz economy and more personal involvement of members in the world market system, though morally and socially the kibbutz way of life is opposed to the dominant forms of competitive market society.

Kibbutz as an Alternative to the City

By the 1920's, there were dozens of urban communes in Mandate Palestine, but in all cases they were relatively small and primarily served as shared households for members who were economically dependent upon the outside labor market. None of them proved strong enough to survive economic and social crises. The kibbutz differed from the rest by moving to an agricultural setting that allowed for the development of a self-managed economy in circumstances that could not have been found at the time in the urban centers. Whether the model developed in the agricultural kibbutz, with its fairly large measure of socioeconomic autonomy, could be sustainable in an urban setting is a question that has not yet been given a definitive answer. Where agriculture emphasized the advantages of socioeconomic and spatial autonomy, industrialization has revealed disadvantages in a number of ways (distance from supply centers, problems of transportation, difficulty in securing prompt repairs and servicing, lack of direct contact with the market).

Initial growth of the kibbutz as primarily an agricultural community received much ideological support from that wing of utopian thought which opposed industrialization and urbanization as going against nature. Many early kibbutz members supported that point of view, saw in agriculture the foundation of their unique way of life, and opposed industrialization of the kibbutz. Paradoxically, members of Degania, who were strong supporters of a small and intimate agricultural community with maximum autarky, were among the first to introduce agricultural machinery into the country. On the other hand, members of Ein Harod openly supported the policy of a large community based on an economy balanced between agriculture, manufacturing and services -- in order to secure maximum autarky. As it turned out, autarky proved impractical and eventually both positions merged under the pressure of events into the policies guiding the contemporary kibbutz.

36

Arthur Ruppin, the chief architect of Jewish settlement, declared in 1925 that the major task of the Zionist Organization was to bring Jews from urban centers abroad to agricultural life in Israel.[1] Ideological support for an "authentic return to the land" came from intellectuals, and particularly among the young. It fitted in with cultural Zionism's view that a physical return to the land as residents was not enough. The main goal should be a revival of national life and creativity, and that could be done best by going back to direct involvement with the natural surroundings. Many of the more gifted young men and women identified with that position, gave up the prospect of urban careers and joined kibbutzim. Within the kibbutzim, new cultural forms were created, including festivals, dances, literature and poetry, many of which have had a major influence in shaping what is unique in contemporary Israeli life.

Furthermore, the kibbutz was the paramount example of the new egalitarian society being formed in Israel under the political hegemony of the labor movement. Manual labor was regarded as a virtue, the kibbutz member was regarded as the highest actualization of the Zionist ideal, and the youth movements educated the elite of the younger generation to forego egoistic careerism in favor of life in a kibbutz. The eminent·Hebrew scholar, S. D. Goitein, then a professor at the Hebrew University, described social conditions of the 1940's and early 1950's as follows: "**Israel is essentially a society without classes** (emphasis in the original-S.M.). No remnants of feudalism, no aristocracy of safely entrenched families, no plutocracy of industrial trusts or business concerns, not even a rule of small bureaucracy as in totalitarian states. .....It is quite natural to find sons - even only sons - of university professors taking up manual work as members of a Kibbutz....."[2]

----

[1] Arthur Ruppin, DIE LANDWIRTSCHAFTLICHE KOLONISATION DER ZIONISTISCHEN ORGANISATION IN PALAESTINA, Aufbau, Berlin, 1925, p. 5.

[2] S. D. Goitein, JEWS AND ARABS, Schocken, New York, 1955, p. 13.

All that changed rapidly as the State of Israel "normalized". Economic development created wealth which in turn brought widening gaps in standards of living and increased social distance. Social values were transformed as technological advances replaced manual labor, and industry replaced agriculture as the basis of the economy. Liberalism replaced socialism and gave ideological justification for the pursuit of self-interest. An academic establishment grew rapidly and influenced a diversion away from the Zionist vision of renewing original Hebrew cultural creativity in favor of integration into European and American cultural trends.

For a time, kibbutz members failed to appreciate fully what was happening. Many of the older members responded by a dogmatic defense of the kibbutz as an agricultural community, as though that were the essence of the kibbutz revolution, even to the point of resisting development of industry or the pursuit of university studies. At the same time, there was considerable ideological confusion in matters of domestic and international politics. A severe crisis ensued, during which time the kibbutz shifted perceptibly to a marginal position on the national scene. Young people in the cities no longer regarded kibbutz life as an ideal, and the youth movements based on Zionist pioneering lost a lot of their membership.

A change began taking place within kibbutzim from the 1960's, as members of the second generation assumed responsible positions in the economic and social spheres, guided by policies more attuned to what was going on in the surrounding society. They promoted an "industrial revolution" which led to rapid expansion of the kibbutz economy. They encouraged higher education and more openness to what was going on in the rest of the country and in the world. Significantly, they did not presume to revive the vision of creating a new Hebrew culture.

Entrance of the second generation into membership in increasingly large numbers was a major factor in bringing about a significant improvement in the kibbutz economy. That led to a rapid rise in the standard of living, and made the kibbutz more attractive to many who were becoming disappointed with urban life. Many singles and young families from the surrounding society applied for membership in a kibbutz. As a result, the kibbutz enjoyed during most of the 1970's and 1980's an unparalleled period of steady growth. It was based primarily on the attractiveness of a rising standard of living attuned to the culture of consumerism, with the multi-generation family and an increased number of children at the center, and not on a firm ideological commitment to older kibbutz principles -- which had become increasingly vague.

The financial crisis of the 1980's affected the entire country, but had a particularly harmful influence on the agricultural sector, and that meant that the kibbutzim were hit harder than most others. In kibbutzim, the crisis brought fundamental issues back to the center of attention and discussion. There was a division of opinion between those who favored a process of "normalization" based on self-interest, including payment for work, and those who favored sticking to the principles of sharing and mutual help while continuing adaptation to constructive changes in the surrounding society.

One of the major decisions facing the kibbutz movement in the 1990's is whether to continue supporting the model of a separate territorial entity, with a large measure of self-government, or to seek a greater measure of integration in the surrounding society. That question has become crucial as limits have been reached for the establishment of additional agricultural settlements. One new direction already being pursued is increased regional cooperation between neighboring kibbutzim, including factories under shared ownership, regional schools and cultural activities, and even joint cultivation of adjoining fields. A further step has been taken through greater integration within the county administration in those regions where kibbutzim are dominant and more or less control county government. As a result, there is now more interaction with the neighboring non-kibbutz population. Furthermore, the trend toward regionalism has weakened the country-wide organization of the kibbutzim in federations, particularly after the poor performance of the TAKAM and Kibbutz Artzi secretariats during the recent financial crisis.

That still leaves open the question of whether the kibbutz could integrate successfully into an urban surrounding, including whatever changes might be required in its legal, physical and organizational structure, as well as in its socioeconomic functioning. By remaining dependent upon territorial autonomy, the kibbutz does limit the possibilities of further growth, while pursuing greater integration at the cost of adaptation opens the way for surrender of the basic principles that distinguish the kibbutz from current market society. Integrating into an urban surrounding would require substantial changes in conception, and surrender of much of the autonomy that the agricultural kibbutz acquired in the past. Success in that direction, though, could open up the way for massive development of "urban kibbutzim", with important consequences for the future. However, for the time being members show little enthusiasm for the prospect of urban kibbutzim and there has been almost no ideological preparation made for such a possible breakthrough.

The question of how far changes can be made in the kibbutz in order to adapt it to new social and economic needs without destroying its essence has now become of vital importance, and is the subject of much discussion. Clearly, a prior condition for conducting a responsible search for an answer, and particularly with reference to urban prospects, is knowledge of past experience.

Urban Background to Communitarian Theory

Urban civilization had its beginnings in the great cities constructed in Western Asia some five thousand years ago. However, most of the cities which we know today in Europe and the Mediterranean area had their origin in the period of the Roman Empire. The Romans initiated establishment of urban centers even in the most distant regions under their control. Those urban centers served two main purposes. One was to provide suitable sites for administrative centers and concentration of military power in order to ensure control of the region. The other purpose was to build a base for expansion of trade in the region and beyond it.

An outstanding achievement of the Roman Empire was development of widespread trading relations on a permanent and organized basis between very distant regions. This trade consisted for the most part of agricultural and craft products. The agricultural producers lived in villages, while the craftsmen and the traders lived in the cities. As the Roman Empire declined, the differences between rural and urban societies became more and more accentuated.

In rural areas, feudal strongmen usurped effective control from the weakened Roman administration, and in the course of time they reduced most of the agricultural population to serfdom or virtual slavery. In the cities, the craftsmen and traders organized in order to ensure continued administrative stability, often using the emerging Church bureaucracy as cooperative allies. Each craft and trading group formed a separate guild, with strict rules for self-regulation, and together they worked out rules for self-government of their city. Those guilds provided the socioeconomic foundation for urban communities based on a distributive economy which moderated harmful influences of the market economy.

In the course of time, every individual belonged to a specific social group that was either a rural or an urban community. Identity of the individual was determined by the group to which he belonged, and there was very little mobility between groups. The rural community was influenced by close involvement in the natural cycles of agricultural production, and the predominance of physical labor. In urban centers, the craft communities were influenced primarily by the character of the skills passed on from generation to generation, and by the need to protect their economic interests through control over the extent and quality of production. As for the trading guilds, their economic interests required monopolistic control over trade and assurance of ethical conduct between traders for the sake of stability and continuity.

Development of the money economy weakened traditional authority and facilitated social mobility from rural to urban centers. Within the cities, large-scale manufacturing replaced skilled craftsmanship and soon the guilds were a vanishing phenomenon. Even the traditionally powerful trading groups found that long years of mutual trust and ethical conduct could not compete with the new methods of financial transactions which gave priority to individual interests over those of the group. The sense of community weakened as the socioeconomic foundation eroded. People swarming into the cities came as individuals. They found themselves without clear group identification, except for their new status as hired workers or proletariat.

In effect, the emergence of what has been called modern society has been most predominantly characterized by a transition from a communal to a individual focus. The negative aspects of social disintegration accompanying this process have been the subject of much discussion, and the desire to mitigate the negative aspects has aroused numerous attempts to restore some viable form of communal life. For the most part, those efforts to revive communal living have either looked backward to lost communities of the past or forward to utopian visions of the future. In most cases, too little attention has been paid to the concrete socioeconomic conditions required for the creation and maintenance of communal life.

Urban Communities

Johannes Althusius was born in Germany in the latter part of the sixteenth century, when urban communities were succumbing to the new order of industrial capitalism. He was a trained jurist, who had been strongly influenced by Aristotelian and Calvinist traditions. Just as Aristotle's treatise on politics was more concerned with the socioeconomic foundations of government than with technical rules of governing, so too the major work by Althusius, written in Latin, bore the title POLITICA[3] but was in reality a treatise intended to defend the guild communities as the proper socioeconomic basis for ideal government. Since he justified much of his theoretical construction on examples taken from the Bible and the communal forms prevalent in ancient Hebrew society, there is more than co-incidental interest in his views for the study of the kibbutz. He noted the central importance of the family in the early Hebrew tribes, the changes which took place during the transition from nomadic to settled town life, the growing influence of commerce, and the role of the elders.

Althusius began his treatise with the assumption that there is a natural inclination among human beings to live together socially for mutual benefit. This he calls "consociatio symbiotica". The primary form of the "consociatio symbiotica" is the family, which is bound together by both conjugal and consanguinal ties. The whole or parts of the extended family may participate at the same time in other or secondary social groups formed on an economic, social or religious basis. He calls this kind of group "consociatio collegarum". Then there is the third kind of social group, the "consociatio universitatis", which provides the comprehensive framework for political union of the other groups. The city at the time of Althusius, and as described by him, was made up of such groups, with the guilds being the foremost example, and a "consociatio universitatis" serving as a comprehensive framework within which the varying interests of the different groups were mediated and shaped into a common policy.

----

[3] Johannes Althusius, POLITICA, editio tertia, Herbornae Nassoviorum, 1614. Reprinted by Scientia, Aalen, 1961. [There is an abridged English translation by F. S. Carney, THE POLITICS OF JOHANNES ALTHUSIUS, Eyre & Spottiswoode, London, 1964.]

By providing a theoretical foundation for the guilds, Althusius made an important contribution to communitarian theory and his work is deserving of more attention than it has received. He was one of the first to explore in detail the unique social structure developed in European cities in the period between the decline of feudalism and the rise of modern nationalism. However, during his life events moved in a direction different from that which he proposed. Socioeconomic changes induced by the industrial revolution soon put his work out of touch with reality, and it vanished from public interest until brought back by the nineteenth century German jurist, Otto von Gierke.

Germany experienced rapid urban and economic growth in the latter part of the nineteenth century as a result of industrialization and development of a market society. Between the years 1850 and 1880, the net national product doubled and the population grew by 40%. The urban population grew at a much faster pace since part of the rural population moved to the cities in search of work and better living conditions. In the course of those thirty years, the population of Berlin grew from 419,000 to 1,122,000, and in most other German cities there were similar or even higher rates of growth.

Otto von Gierke, professor of jurisprudence, deplored the emergence in urban centers of mass society based on individuals with no organic bonds, with only money transactions and conflicting interests as the basis of their interaction. He looked back with nostalgia on the ethical bonds which guided conduct of the old trading communities, of which the Hansa League was a dominant example. In 1868, he published the first of a series of books on traditional communities in Germany, with extensive argument that the old communal or corporate structure of society is more appropriate to authentic German culture. Ten years later, he published the first full-length study of Johannes Althusius[4], whom he saw as a forerunner to his own views. For Gierke, the choice was between the mass

----

[4] Otto von Gierke, DAS DEUTSCHE GENOSSENSCHAFTSRECHT, Berlin, 1868. [There is an abridged English translation by M. Fischer, COMMUNITY IN HISTORICAL PERSPECTIVE, Cambridge Univ. Press, 1990.] JOHANNES ALTHUSIUS UND DIE ENTWICKLUNG DER NATURRECHTLICHEN STAATSTHEORIEN, Breslau, 1878.

society of the emerging individual industrial cities, with nothing standing between the individual and the State, or a return to a corporate structure with each individual being a part of some community and the State as co-ordinator of the various communities. He recognized that the old communal structure had broken down, but held that it could and must be rebuilt.

For Gierke, the traditional German community rested on ethical standards and mutual help. The individual was a part of the larger group, and had a clear identity. In contrast, the emerging capitalist market society made self-interest more important than ethical standards; the individual was separated from his social group and lost his unique identity; and in the end the uprooted individual was left to fend for himself in a mass society instead of having the benefits of mutual help. Gierke lamented development of modern society as a decline and not as an advance to higher levels of civilization. According to him, the magnificent ethical spirit of commerce exemplified by the Hansa League had turned into a degraded shopkeeper mentality, and emergence of the absolute State was matched by emergence of the absolute individual. The concept of community had become almost entirely lost.

Less than a decade after Gierke's first major work appeared, Ferdinand Toennies published a study of the contrast between the dying rural community governed by the norms of a traditional culture, and the emerging urban mass market society that was increasingly governed by a bureaucracy. The book was destined to have a powerful influence on several generations of social thinkers.[5] Toennies, who had grown up in the rural area of northwest Germany, described with nostalgia the traditional community based on family and having the home as its center. That basic community or Gemeinschaft then expanded to include neighbors within the surrounding territory, and was further re-enforced by participation in a shared culture of normative behavior and values. At the bottom of this contrast stood a metaphysical opposition between the natural rural community, rooted in the soil, and the rational social order of market society.

----

[5] Ferdinand Toennies, GEMEINSCHAFT UND GESELLSCHAFT, Berlin, 1887 [English translation by C. Loomis, COMMUNITY AND ASSOCIATION, Routledge, Kegan Paul, London, 1955; and under the title COMMUNITY AND SOCIETY, Michigan State University, 1957].

Toennies believed that natural community (Gemeinschaft), formed around the household, is possible in small towns as well as in villages where it is possible to maintain neighborliness and direct personal relations; but he rejected emphatically the possibility that natural communities could survive in the new market society (Gesellschaft) of industrial cities. His work gave powerful impetus to an idealization of rural communities, added forcefully to the romantic criticism of massive urban growth, and offered to the public a handy phrase to describe with facility a complicated process of change in the character of human relations within the socioeconomic conditions emerging out of the industrial revolution.

Chapter Five
COMMUNITY IN A MARKET SOCIETY (II)

Though Martin Buber grew up in rural Poland, he was not particularly impressed by the virtues of the traditional Jewish community there. What did make a strong impression on him was the comradeship which characterized the Hasidic groups. As he watched them, he experienced the sense of togetherness which overcame individualistic and selfish barriers, and seemed to raise each participant to a higher level of being. Later, he learned of the young Zionists who dedicated themselves to renewing Hebrew life in Palestine by changing the socioeconomic conditions there through their own participation, and first of all by changing themselves. He was strongly attracted by that pioneering spirit, and also by the moral views of Aaron David Gordon, one of their leaders. The early communes and kibbutzim seemed to him to be a possible realization of a new kind of community, based on spiritual comradeship similar to that of the Hasidic group.

Buber had earlier been influenced by the Lebensphilosophie of his teachers, Wilhelm Dilthey and Georg Simmel, and that approach was further strengthened by his reading of Nietzsche and Bergson. He was impressed by Toennies' critical view of individualistic market society and by his favorable exposition of Gemeinschaft. Then he came under the direct influence of Gustav Landauer, who won him over to the cause of anarchistic communes.

In a lecture given during that period, Buber attempted to combine the theories of Toennies and Landauer by explaining that the origin of community was in the natural development of the family, on the basis of shared possessions, and particularly joint ownership of land. However, society had evolved beyond that stage and it was no longer possible to return to a natural community. Instead, the alternative to mass market society was spiritual community, or more accurately, community based on Erlebnis that builds comradeship of a personal or group character. In another lecture of that time, given in 1920 at a meeting of Labor Zionists, Buber stressed that community is based on sharing, and that Toennies was right to emphasize the importance of natural sharing, but insisted that it was time to go beyond Toennies and to realize that even more important was the shared goal. He contrasted the organic life of community with the mechanical life of market society, and went on to describe the Zionist pioneers building kibbutzim in Palestine as pioneers of organic socialism in the contemporary world.[1]

In 1922, Hermann Schmalenbach, who was one of Buber's close personal friends, published a seminal article[2] in which he took issue with Toennies' central thesis by asserting that the latter's conception of community (Gemeinschaft) was not realistic. Toennies had found community in the traditional pattern, where its "bases are the natural, genuine, and indeed physical forms of solidarity: consanguinity and proximity -- kinship and neighborhood". However, contended Schmalenbach, that is no longer the case. Now, "young people tear themselves away from the parental home and parental life style,.....they storm out into the free and open spaces of the world, and ..... they join themselves together in friendship groups, which they themselves like to call 'communities'". But, for Schmalenbach, these youth groups did not form communities in the original sense of Gemeinschaft as developed by Toennies. Therefore, he originated a different term and called the youth group a Bund or communion as distinguished from community.

----

[1] Apparently the above two lectures, originally delivered in German, have been published only in Hebrew translations. They appeared in the monthly periodical, MAABAROT, vol. 2, nos. 2 and 3, 1920.

[2] Hermann Schmalenbach, "Die Soziologishe Kategorie des Bundes," DIE DIOSKUREN: JAHRBUCH FUER GEISTESWISSENSCHAFTEN, I, 1922, pp. 35-105. A partial English translation was published in the collective work, THEORIES OF SOCIETY, edited by Talcott Parsons et al., Free Press, New York, 1961, pp. 331-347. A complete translation appeared in a collection of Schmalenbach's articles, ON SOCIETY AND EXPERIENCE, edited and translated by G. Lueschen and G. P. Stone, University of Chicago Press, 1977, pp. 64-125.

Toennies had defined Gemeinschaft in terms of three kinds of sharing: family, territory and culture. What Schmalenbach did was to remove the family, and leave the community resting only on shared space and consciousness. By removing the natural element of the family, Schmalenbach hoped to adapt the Bund to conditions of market society (Gesellschaft) characterized by social mobility, while preserving the traditional values of Gemeinschaft in terms of shared living both physically and ideologically. However, the difference is of vital importance. A natural or familial bond determines personal identity of a permanent and non-voluntary order, while spatial and ideological connections are intrinsically changeable. For Toennies, Gemeinschaft was a permanent relationship passed on from generation to generation, while for Schmalenbach a Bund was a temporary group which could be formed or cease to exist at any time.

Buber's attempts during the 1920's to strengthen community by substituting a strongly spiritual relationship for the ideological one only obscured the basic problem. In 1930, he gave an extended exposition of his views in an important lecture[3] in which he avoided the term "Bund" and instead used the more philosophically compatible "Lebensgemeinschaft", a term which suggested a position between Toennies and Schmalenbach, and perhaps it was in order to disassociate himself from the somewhat controversial use of the term Bund by Hans Blueher. In his address, Buber sought to contrast the natural or organic basis of Gemeinschaft, favored by romantic criticism of technology and industrialization, with mechanical society identified with Gesellschaft. He sought to give a new turn to Toennies' argument by distinguishing between groups formed on the basis of shared life as against groups formed on the basis of shared interests.

Buber defined the group based on shared life as Lebensgemeinschaft, in contrast to the group based on shared interests which he saw as Gesellschaft. In earlier times, the family was the outstanding example of a group based on shared life or Lebensgemeinschaft, Buber claimed, but modern society brought the family to a state of crisis and diminution.

----

[3] Martin Buber, "Wie kann Gemeinschaft werden?", KAMPF UM ISRAEL, Schocken, Berlin, 1933, pp. 252-280.

What was needed was a new foundation of shared life by groups building their lives together in a spirit of brotherhood, **as though they were families**. Significantly, in the lecture he made no reference to Toennies but did refer to Max Weber's distinction between Vergemeinschaftung and Vergesellschaftung.

Community and the Primary Group

American society north of the Mexican border has had almost no direct experience with traditional communities in the sense of Gemeinschaft. According to common European usage, the term "community" generally means a pattern of continuing relations on a person-to-person basis, usually arising out of shared kinship, shared ethnic identity, shared residential area, or some shared activities that give rise to a "community of interests" of a more permanent nature. Within American culture, personal relations in the past have tended to be relatively more superficial, primarily due to a much greater degree of social mobility. As a result, communal ties in northern America have tended to remain on a superficial level, and even remote from the diluted version of Lebensgemeinschaft suggested by Buber.

The American sociologist, Edward Shils, made one of the more serious attempts to grapple with this subject. He read the German sociological literature, as well as the French and British, made interesting observations, and in the end came back to the phenomenon best understood by American sociology--the primary group as studied and conceptually formulated in the pioneering work of Charles Cooley.[4] In the first of the articles cited here, Shils defined the primary group as characterized by "a high degree of solidarity, informality in the code of rules which regulate the behavior of its members, and autonomy in the creation of these rules". He made only passing reference to Toennies and Schmalenbach, and devoted most

----

[4] Edward Shils, "The Study of the Primary Group", THE POLICY SCIENCES, edited by D. Lerner and H. D. Lasswell, Stanford University Press, 1951, pp. 44-69; "Primordial, Personal, Sacred and Civil Ties", BRITISH JOURNAL OF SOCIOLOGY, 1957, pp. 130-145; and a collection of articles entitled, THE CONSTITUTION OF SOCIETY, University of Chicago Press, 1982.

of his discussion to research on the primary group within the context of industrial psychology. In the second article, he gave a more profound review of the background, with particular attention to the contribution by Schmalenbach (and no reference to Buber). He made a clear distinction between Toennies' Gemeinschaft and Schmalenbach's Bund, with an interpretation that made the Bund into a primary group in the sense conventionally understood in American sociology.

According to Shils, the essential element in the Bund is solidarity and not what is used to express that solidarity. People form a Bund or primary group because they want solidarity, and can use a wide variety of means to achieve it. Neither common territory, kinship, workplace or ideology are necessary components, but each or all of them can be used as means to achieve solidarity. In the long run, though, the bonds that unite the primary group are communicated through consciousness of them as formulated in some form of code or symbols, and most coherently in an ideology.

Between Theory and the Existing Kibbutz

As shown in the following chapter, empirical research of the kibbutz in Israel has developed on the background of theoretical formulations ranging ambiguously from Lebensgemeinschaft and Bund to primary group. There has been considerable confusion in the use of the term "community", as well as about the role of ideology in the face of different and even conflicting ideologies that have produced very similar kibbutzim. Shared territory, kinship, workplace and goals are important contributing factors in making the contemporary kibbutz what it is, and all produce a sense of solidarity. Yet none of them seem to explain what keeps the kibbutz going as an alternative way of life in a world where the dominant trends are toward greater individualism and more flexible primary groups.

The kibbutz was created by individuals working within primary groups that had many of the attributes of Schmalenbach's Bund. They accepted the conventional criticism of urban market society as expressed in the code word, "Gesellschaft", and wanted the kibbutz to pioneer the way in building a better and more just society. Some attempts were made to integrate the kibbutz into urban surroundings in the spirit of Lebensgemeinschaft or Bund but they did not succeed, and apparently they were not taken too seriously by those within and without the early kibbutzim. There was at best only a slight tendency toward syndicalism among urban workers, that produced at best some cooperatives, and hardly a fertile field for real community. The economic interest of the worker in his paycheck proved stronger than any revolutionary desire to change the structure of society. Preference was given to building strong labor unions adapted to conditions of the market society.

While kibbutz members played an important role in forming the early socialist parties and the General Federation of Labor (Histadrut), the fundamental differences between the utopian socialism of the kibbutz and the economistic labor unionism of the urban worker eventually led to estrangement between them, and weakened the Israeli labor movement. Siegfrid Landshut, discussed in the following chapter, gave an early warning of the danger, but his advice was not heeded. In his book on the kibbutz, he pointed out that socioeconomically the kibbutz was already "after the revolution" and had built a classless society in which conflicting economic interests were abolished. Therefore, the members were free to concern themselves with general objectives and especially those of the Zionist or national movement. That also led kibbutz members to participate in party politics on the basis of more extremist ideological positions, and particular in favor of "class warfare", even though that had little direct bearing on themselves. Most of the urban workers were satisfied with piece-meal gains and social democracy of the kind represented by MAPAI, and rejected the radical socialism with which the majority of kibbutz members identified. There was also the nagging problem of hired labor in kibbutzim, that placed the economic interests of the kibbutzim in opposition to the economic interests of the worker, and brought the reality of class differences into the kibbutz itself with the members in a position contradicting their ideology.

Since establishment of the State of Israel the extent of hired labor in kibbutzim, and particularly in regional plants, has grown in proportions and resulted in serious antagonism. Kibbutz members have not been able to find a satisfactory solution to their ideological dilemma. They need the hired labor (which comes to about ten percent of the total labor force in the kibbutz economy), but do not know how to handle relations with the hired workers except on a purely capitalist basis of the "cash nexus".

Kibbutzim introduced directly into an urban surrounding would presumably engage in economic activities that would attract hired labor, and the resulting tensions would make integration of those kibbutzim into their social environment difficult and perhaps impossible. As it is, a more intensive involvement of the kibbutz in the surrounding market economy has given rise in the 1990's to a questioning of basic principles, and what could rightly be called an ideological crisis.

Part of that ideological crisis arises out of ambiguous commitment to root values, and an all too often occurrence of verbal declarations that stand in blatant contrast to facts in the field of action. Curiously enough, some of the major social science research done in kibbutzim has supported that ambiguity by unintentionally giving greater attention to the phenomenological dimension while neglecting empirical data, or in concentrating more on members' opinions than on facts.

Furthermore, as can be seen in the following chapter, the theoretical work of Buber, Schmalenbach and Shils has been used as background for influential professional studies of the kibbutz, even though their theories were developed in a different cultural context and without demonstrating that they are relevant to the specific conditions of the kibbutz and its social surroundings. Since actual development of the kibbutz has not moved in directions anticipated by those theories, the unavoidable conclusion is that results of such research must be studied with reservations.

Chapter Six
APPLICATION OF THEORY IN EMPIRICAL RESEARCH

Buber left Germany in 1938 and took up an appointment as professor of social philosophy at the Hebrew University in Jerusalem, where he met another refugee from Germany, Siegfrid Landshut, who had similar interests. Landshut had studied philosophy and sociology, been appointed lecturer at Hamburg University, and edited the first German edition of Marx's early writings (DIE FRUEHSCHRIFTEN), that introduced to a wider audience the previously unknown philosophical discussion of alienation by the young Marx. In 1933, after the Nazi regime exluded Jews from teaching in the universities, he had left Germany for Palestine.

Under the influence of Buber and Arthur Ruppin, Landshut spent a year in a kibbutz and then published the first full-scale social study on the basis of field work. It remains one of the best and deepest studies of the kibbutz, despite the many changes that have taken place through the years. Landshut wrote his report in German. It was then translated into Hebrew and eventually published in 1944.[1] Initial reception was cool and the book had very limited circulation, both because there was at the time little academic interest in the kibbutz and because its objectively critical approach went against the grain of the prevalent ideological support and admiration for the kibbutz.

----

[1] Siegfrid Landshut, HAKVUTZAH, Zionist Library, Jerusalem, 1944.
Copies of the German typescript are in the libraries of Hamburg University and Yad Tabenkin. An earlier book giving a broad socioeconomic analysis of the kibbutz was published nine years earlier by a Swiss citizen, Joseph Weiss, who had not been to Palestine and based his doctoral dissertation on published data and personal communications. It was published under the title, DIE "KWUZAH", Bern, 1935, and is a rich source of factual data for the early period.

Landshut's study of the kibbutz begins with a review of communitarian experiments in the past, and particularly the communes formed in the United States in the 19th century. He observed that social groups have lived together either on the basis of kinship or ideological affiliation. Kinship groups have been either tribal or extended households, but these are no longer found in developed societies and in any event have not provided the basis for recent communal experiments. Those ideologies which have provided the basis for communal living have been either religious or secular. Empirical observation shows that of the two the religious communes have had greater endurance and have lasted for longer periods of time, though altogether communal experiments have been almost wholly a failure.

He then went on to describe how the kibbutz was formed, its distinctive features, its ideology, its organizational structure, its economy, its society, and its place in the Zionist policy of settlement. In addition to presenting much pertinent empirical data, he made a number of penetrating observations about kibbutz life which are still valid today, and continue to make his book important.

Of significance for the present discussion is the clear division drawn by Landshut between natural or kinship communities and those formed on the basis of shared ideology. He classified the kibbutz in the latter category, and discussed the limited role allowed to the family. In the original German manuscript, the term used by Landshut to describe the kibbutz is Lebensgemeinschaft, in the way used by Buber, rather than the more general term of Gemeinschaft in the sense of Toennies, or the more specific term of Bund used by Schmalenbach. Among other things, he pointed out the contradiction inherent between community of comradeship and authentic family life; as well as the contradiction existing between the socialist commitment of the kibbutz to solidarity with the workers and their class interests (referred to at the end of the previous chapter), though at the same time the kibbutz as a revolutionary community had already made the transition to a post-revolutionary social order without class interests.

Conditions were difficult at the time that Landshut conducted his research. He found the kibbutz involved in a crisis situation, with its ideology in need of reorientation in the light of new circumstances and its economy unable to support the rapid growth in population and the added burden of sheltering refugees from Europe. Landshut, using his considerable experience in ideological research, was able to point out serious weaknesses.

Of fundamental importance was the enduring dilemma betwen conflicting interpretations of the kibbutz as a means or an end. If the kibbutz was only a community of comradeship formed ideologically on the basis of a common goal (such as Schmalenbach's Bund), presumably it would have no further reason for existence once the goal was secured. The kibbutz was formed as part of the Zionist endeavor to resettle the Hebrew people in its historical homeland, but what would happen once that objective was achieved? Within the kibbutz there was a never-ending debate between those who saw the kibbutz only as a means for realizing the Zionist program, and those who found a deeper purpose in also creating a new and better way of life. Landshut reached sceptical conclusions about the future of the kibbutz, and that did not endear him to the ideological leadership. The debate assumed critical proportions after establishment of the State of Israel when many members left the kibbutz on the assumption that their job was done and they could return to "normal" society. Most, though, chose to carry on the revolution in the hope of expanding its scope to a larger public.

Debate Over the Family

At this time, in 1951, an American anthropologist and his wife did a year of field-work in one of the veteran kibbutzim, which they called Kiryat Yedidim in their research reports.[2] That kibbutz was, at the time, almost thirty years old. Most of the members had come from Poland or parts of the old Austro-Hungarian Empire, and they had been deeply influenced by Buber and the wider ideology of revolutionary "community of comradeship". Spiro caught the message, was much impressed by the anti-familial atmosphere prevailing in the community of comradeship, and failed to appreciate that formation of a familial foundation was in fact already well under way. At the time of his field work, Kiryat Yedidim had close to 100 families and almost 200 children.

---

[2] Melford E. Spiro, KIBBUTZ: VENTURE IN UTOPIA, Harvard University Press, 1956; CHILDREN OF THE KIBBUTZ, Harvard University Press, 1958.

Spiro commented on the measures taken to curb familial influence, and went so far as to call the kibbutz as a whole one large family in opposition to a community made up of families. Under the early influence of his stay in the kibbutz, he went on to publish a sensational article which attracted widespread attention because it claimed that the kibbutz was a society without families according to the definition established by George Murdock. A more plausible case could have been made to show on the basis of kibbutz evidence that Murdock's definition was erroneous. Some years later, after a return visit to Kiryat Yedidim, Spiro retracted his earlier position. Clearly he had been influenced unduly by what the members had said, and had given insufficient weight to what they were doing. Bruno Bettelheim made the same mistake some years later in his best-selling, CHILDREN OF THE DREAM.

One of Buber's most prominent disciples within the kibbutz movement, Menahem Gerson, tried to adjust the dominant anti-familialistic ideology to the facts in the field by acknowledging existence of the family, but pointed out that in the kibbutz the family is based on comradeship rather than forming a separate socioeconomic entity. He answered Spiro's thesis by acknowledging "that the family is a very significant social and educational force in kibbutz life, and the cohesion between the different generations of a family ..... is a very strong one". He went on to explain that the particular family is not an economic unit, but is economically inseparable from the larger community and the children are aware of their economic dependence on the community rather than on their parents. The parents are deeply involved in the education of their children, but do so in the system of collective education through partnership with professional educators from the time the children are born, and with participation of the entire community. These points are precisely where Murdock's definition fails to hold water, and where Spiro made his mistake.[3]

----

[3] George Peter Murdock, SOCIAL STRUCTURE, Macmillan, New York, 1949. Melford E. Spiro, "Is the Family Universal?", AMERICAN ANTHROPOLOGIST, Vol. 56, 1954, pp. 839-846; SEX AND GENDER, Duke University Press, 1979. Menahem Gerson, "Family Problems in the Kibbutz", CHILDREN IN COLLECTIVES, ed. by P. B. Neubauer, Springfield, 1965, p. 233.

Yonina Talmon, who had studied with Buber at the Hebrew University, undertook to lead an extensive research program on the kibbutz that began in 1955 and continued for a decade[4]. She headed a team of sociologists who based their study of the kibbutz more on questionnaires than on study of the empirical facts. On the basis of answers collected and collateral observations, she arrived at a theoretical formulation according to which the kibbutz begins as a primary group unified by a common ideological goal, common emotional experience, and direct human relations -- more or less the attributes stressed by Schmalenbach and Buber, and further refined by Edward Shils. However, as the kibbutz population grows, it becomes less homogeneous. With the absorption of new members, the age differential increases and frequently new members come from a different background. The new members have not been participants in the intense emotional experience of founding members who settled on the land, ploughed the first furrow and initiated the new way of life, though they share a common ideology. More formal organization is needed in order to keep the community functioning in an orderly and agreed manner, but the process of institutionalization leads to further weakening or neutralization of the primary group.

Meanwhile, couples form and children are born. At that stage, tensions develop between the community as a whole and the nuclear family unit, as well as between both of them and the institutional structure. In order to survive, the community must find a way to resolve continuing social problems in a stable way. That requires moving from the stage of relatively simple solidarity in the primary group to recognized pluralism of at least several primary groups, along with significant differentials in age, background and views. Talmon described this development of the kibbutz as a progression from Bund to Commune.

Emphasis in the process of development varies from kibbutz to kibbutz. According to Talmon, there are three basic possibilities in the growth of a kibbutz. In the first of these, the social connection remains dominant. Social groups are formed by people who work in the same place or branch, have children of the same age, have a similar background, or happen to

----

[4] Yonina Talmon, FAMILY AND COMMUNITY IN THE KIBBUTZ, Harvard University Press, 1972.

have similar hobbies. In that direction, maximum efforts are made to restrain familial influences and maintain the unified character of the community as a social body with the emphasis on comradeship. This requires stronger administrative efforts to maintain routine life on a stable and agreed basis. At the next stage, institutionalization of kibbutz life comes to dominate the face-to-face relations which characterized the Bund, and which were considered by Buber to be essential for successful communal living.

The second possible direction is the emergence of strong family units and the consequent preference of members for familial rather than social relations. The nuclear or expanded family becomes the focal point in building day-to-day life. There is less reliance on the administration and more emphasis placed on arrangements made within the family circle. At such a stage, the family units become a threat to the unity and solidarity of the community.

The third possible direction is described by Talmon as a kind of aberration. It occurs when factions are formed. At that stage, the kibbutz becomes a kind of coalition of sectorial interests. She assumed that conflict between the various sectorial interests usually leads to dissolution of the Commune.

Erik Cohen, one of Talmon's collaborators, has carried her work forward by defining another stage in development of the kibbutz. He contends that the process of differentiation eventually leads from the Commune to a form which he calls Association, and which he equates with Toennies' Gesellschaft.[5] According to Cohen, increased professionalism leads to strengthening of the administration and weakening of direct participation in decision- making by most kibbutz members. Life becomes

----

[5] Erik Cohen, "Progress and Communality: Value Dilemmas in the Collective Movement", INTERNATIONAL REVIEW OF COMMUNITY DEVELOPMENT, 1966, pp. 3-18; "The Structural Transformation of the Kibbutz", SOCIAL CHANGE, edited by G. K. Zollschan and W. Hirsch, Schenkman, Cambridge, Mass., 1976, pp. 703-742; "The Israeli Kibbutz-- The Dynamics of Pragmatic Utopianism", TOTALITARIAN DEMOCRACY AND AFTER, Magnes, Jerusalem, 1984, pp. 362-376.

more routinized as the kibbutz becomes a permanent way-of-life. This phenomenon he calls the transition to Association.

Menachem Rosner, himself a veteran kibbutz member and a participant in the research group led by Yonina Talmon, agrees with Cohen and sees weakening of social solidarity in the kibbutz as the main problem. He sees comradeship as an essential element in building the kibbutz, and has been critical of familialism as a weakening trend. In a number of articles[6], Rosner has identified the central problem as that of alienation. According to him, the kibbutz in its initial period overcame alienation (in the Marxist sense) by creating a free association of producers. In further development of his view, Rosner departs from the Marxian concept of alienation connected with production and stresses the relationship between weakening comradeship and growing social alienation as a major problem in the contemporary kibbutz. His position, influenced by Buber and the "community of comrades" school, tends to ignore the view that the weakening of youthful comradeship is a natural process in a maturing social group that has become in large measure a natural community on a firm familial basis. His work is characterized by continued inclination to emphasis the importance of comradeship for kibbutz success, and critical judgment of familialism as a divisive influence on the community. Like Erik Cohen, he has interpreted change in the kibbutz negatively as a continual and retrogressive movement from community to association in the spirit of Gemeinschaft to Gesellschaft.

So far, Talmon, Cohen and Rosner have been among the most widely published and publicized social researchers of the kibbutz, after Spiro. While they have done much to bring the kibbutz to the attention of the academic world, their work suffers from two serious faults, one methodological and one theoretical. From the methodological point of view, their system of questionnaires given to a sample population is not different in principle from ordinary public opinion surveys. It bases the frame of reference on what people think and say rather than on what they do.

----

[6] For example, Menachem Rosner, "The Kibbutz Between Re-Alienation and De-Alienation", **COMMUNAL LIFE** edited by Y. Gorni et al., Yad Tabenkin, Efal, and Transaction Publishers, New Brunswick, 1987, pp. 431-439.

Such research can explore the subjective or phenomenological aspects of social life, but is a poor source for hard empirical evidence. That is an important limitation, and one all too characteristic of a kind of sociological research that has aroused justifiable criticism. As Marx has shown convincingly, a study of the socioeconomic facts (and foremost how people cope in practice with existential needs) is a necessary prior condition for an understanding of the phenomenological sphere.

The other serious fault is that, like the earlier work by Spiro, Talmon and her colleagues missed the central importance of the family in the positive development of kibbutz community. True, at the time of their major research project overt public opinion in most of the kibbutzim was still largely anti-familialistic, and as yet relatively few of the second generation had entered into the main stream of kibbutz life. However, a study of the demographic facts would have revealed what questionnaires could not show, that the anti-familialistic ideology of the veteran members had been formed by past life experience, mostly in their childhood and in a different cultural context. Socioeconomic conditions within the kibbutz were already changing rapidly, and the dominant ideological view of the family was soon to undergo a profound change. Support for familialism became increasingly strong and public as members from the second generation became more prominent both in numbers and in influence. Just a few years after conclusion of the research led by Talmon, familialism had become a part of majority public opinion or consensus in most kibbutzim, multi-generation families were a dominant part of the social structure, and sleeping arrangements for the children began shifting to the parental apartments.

As it has turned out, the family is not a divisive element and does not destroy solidarity of the community. On the contrary, as proven under the stress of the recent financial crisis, family bonds have contributed more than anything else to keeping the kibbutzim together and preventing a significant flight of members (as would most probably have happened had the kibbutz been only a "community of comrades"). Furthermore, the social and familial dimensions have proven to be mutually supportive and not oppositional. The unique structure of the kibbutz as a communal household has permitted all of the young who wish to remain to do so. Since at least half do so, the result has been expansion of family units to three or four generations.

In contrast to what happens in contemporary market societies, almost every child born in a kibbutz now grows up alongside grandparents who live in the same communal household. That "organic" development has been balanced dialectically by significantly increased individual freedom. One important reason for this is the strong sense of rootedness and personal security that characterizes the second generation. Unlike the first generation, they are not afraid that the kibbutz might collapse if the bonds of solidarity are not maintained by suppressing individualism. They want to expand their social and cultural horizons, and bring their own potentialities to maximum realization. They see growth of the individual as a means for strengthening the community, and not as a disintegrative process.

Chapter Seven
ROLE OF THE FAMILY

There are two kinds of extended family, the natural or consanguinal and the socioeconomic. The distinction between the two was made quite clearly by Aristotle in his *Politics* , where he describes progression from the natural family to the socioeconomic family. The word "progression" is used here deliberately, because Aristotle saw the emergence of the socioeconomic family out of the natural family as a definite sign of human progress toward a higher order of being. For him, the socioeconomic unit, or the *oikos*, was already the incipient State and the mark of civilization or rational order. Similarly among the Romans, there was a progression from the early *gens*, or clan based on direct descent from a common ancestor, to the *familia*, which resembled the Greek *oikos* and included servants and others within an extended household.

The situation was somewhat different in early Hebrew society, since all Hebrews were recognized as having Abraham as their common ancestor. The primary familial grouping, or *beyt-av*, was an integral part of the *mishpaha* or clan, which in turn was part of the *shevet* or tribe. However, persons who came from elsewhere, either from another tribe or another cultural group, and who integrated socioeconomically into the local way of life and its belief-pattern, were accepted as part of the family. Foreigners were those who retained distinct customs and beliefs, and they were excluded from sacrificial ceremonies within the family circle.

An early reference to this distinction among the Hebrews is found in *Exodus* 12.43-48, where only consanguinal members of the larger family, the community of Israel, and others who have been circumcised, may participate in the feast of Passover. They, alone, belonged to the family in the proper sense. Throughout most of the Bible there is a continuing reference to the problem of maintaining consanguinal primacy and restraining socioeconomic influence. Tension between the two orders became severe after the establishment of the monarchy, with the clans and the clan-system in almost constant resistance to the growing political and economic strength of the State. Friction between the "natural" clan pattern of relations and the "organized" political structure continued to be a part of Hebrew culture until the collapse of political independence. Primacy of the natural or consanguinal family then reasserted itself among the dispersed Hebrews, and remained the dominant order in their social living until the rise of the modern state based on the market society. The traditional community, which characterized Jewish existence in the Dispersion for more than a thousand years, was neither a political entity nor a socioeconomic entity in the Greek sense of **polis.** Rather, it provided an instrument for cooperation and mutual help between natural families, and served as their collective representative before the established authority in the surrounding society.

These distinctions are important for a proper understanding of social developmenmt in the kibbutz. Founding members of early kibbutzim were for the most part young, single, and immersed in "modern culture". That is to say, their thinking was deeply influenced by the emerging market society that was rapidly strengthening the socioeconomic order at the expense of the natural family. Since most of these young people identified with revolutionary thinking, and wished to be in the forefront of social change, they favored a dominant role for an egalitarian socioeconomic system of comradeship and suppression of the natural family -- in the name of rebellion against the socioeconomic order of the market society!

Kadish Luz, one of the founding members of Kibbutz Degania Bet, declared in 1923, "kibbutz society does away with private property.....it also does away with the most important institution of capitalist society.....it does away with the institution of the family." He went on to explain that organization of the family as an economic unit in capitalist society gives to the head of the family a kind of control which reduces other members of the family to something like his possessions. Organization of the kibbutz as a socioeconomic unit was intended to liberate each and every person, adults and children, for a life of free association and individual self-realization.

Ideology and Reality

An entire ideology developed around the conception voiced by Kadish Luz and other founding members of like mind, which was then cultivated in the youth movements as a part of basic kibbutz ideology. Free association of adult members and collective education of the children became the accepted and declared pattern of kibbutz life. Much effort was devoted to preventing or weakening overt familial solidarity, since it was interpreted as threatening socioeconomic solidarity. During a certain period of time, the Hebrew term *meshek*, which is roughly equivalent to *oikos*, became more commonly used than the term kibbutz (social grouping). Deliberate stress was placed on the shared socioeconomic framework and its ideological counterpart, and this trend was reinforced by each wave of new members who came out of the youth movements imbued with the spirit of comradeship.

However, as both Plato and Aristotle pointed out, a system of comradeship with completely shared possessions cannot work unless there is also complete sharing of wives and anonymous parenthood with regard to the children. These conditions were rejected by kibbutz members at a very early stage, if at all considered. Already within the first years, small family groups began to emerge, couples displayed marked preference for stable and enduring relations, and between themselves and their children developed intense personal involvement and solidarity. The freedom from economic entanglements provided by the unique kibbutz structure as a communal household allowed the natural family to reach strong personal bonds of attachment.

Within a relatively short time, mostly within the first decade, there was a metamorphosis in each kibbutz of young and single revolutionaries into parents devoted to raising their children and building the shared household on a permanent and stable basis. An essential condition for the establishment of a successful kibbutz was and remains formation of a stratum of families that becomes the continuing social foundation of the community, and which soon becomes the major source of further growth of the kibbutz. In the past, this transformation has not been easy. Dogmatic ideological defense of egalitarian comradeship as the essence of kibbutz life often delayed or complicated the emergence of family life, and even in the 1980's there were still members who saw "familialism" as a threat to kibbutz social solidarity rather than as its chief source of strength.

The period of significant "social take-off" in the kibbutz movement as a whole was during the years 1938-1949, when many of the existing kibbutzim were founded. At that early stage, most kibbutz members were in the age of fertility, and not surprisingly the rate of growth from natural reproduction soon reached 5% annually, which is quite high for any society. Although there was a continuous stream of newcomers from the youth movements and elsewhere, natural reproduction was then and has continued to be the major source of population growth in the kibbutz movement for the past fifty years or more.

During those same years, tens of thousands of persons passed through the kibbutzim, some staying for only days or weeks and other for months or years. For much of the 1930's and 1940's, kibbutzim served as reception centers for refugees from Europe and elsewhere. Most of the newcomers had no intention of joining a kibbutz permanently, and they left as soon as they found work in the surrounding society. According to a report given in 1939 by Israel Bar-Yehuda, then Secretary of the Kibbutz Hameuhad, more than 4,000 adults had left that movement during the preceding four years, with about 80% of them remaining in kibbutzim less than a year -- and many of them only a number of days. At about the same time, Landshut estimated that the average length of stay in a kibbutz on the part of the transient population was a year and a quarter. This transient population imposed a heavy burden on available housing, services and economic means, and seriously impeded development of a stable familial atmosphere within most kibbutzim.

From Camp to Home

In those years of dedication to fulfilling national tasks, kibbutzim were like semi-military camps mostly made up of tents or wooden huts centered around the communal kitchen and dining room. Their members were primarily manpower reserves ready at all times to meet the changing national needs of the hour. After establishment of the independent State of Israel, most of such functions were transferred to the governmental administration. The kibbutzim turned to the challenge of building a permanent way-of-life, with the kibbutz becoming a real home for both adults and children. The quality of housing rapidly improved, along with the general standard of living. More attention was paid to furnishing the familial apartment, and to providing for the children. Soon a strong demand developed to end the system of separate housing for the children and to transfer them to their parents' apartment. The most vocal proponents of the change were young mothers of the second generation, who had themselves been born and raised in a kibbutz and now emphatically rejected the practice of separate sleeping arrangements for their children. Kibbutzim began moving over to family sleeping arrangements for the children in the 1960's, and by the end of the 1980's in almost all of them the children were sleeping in the parental apartment.

Older kibbutzim have shown a surprising degree of vitality. Many members recall the precedent of communes in 19th century America, whose members aged while the younger generation left for better prospects elsewhere, and there have been persistent fears that a similar process may overtake the kibbutzim. Observers from outside frequently raise the issue and lament the departure of the young. In practice, the younger generation continue to be a major source of adult population growth, along with their marriage partners from outside. It turns out in practice that kibbutzim, unlike individual persons, do not age and die away. The more veteran among them already have an active fourth generation and are going on to a fifth. Each succeeding generation brings new life and character to the kibbutz, within a continual process of change. The strong familial bonds that form within the multi-generational families reinforce the ties of solidarity felt by all those who share the communal household.

An overwhelming majority of the current kibbutz population is concentrated in kibbutzim that were founded prior to 1950, and now have a typical family pattern of at least three generations. Between one quarter to one half of their members have been born and raised in the kibbutz. Together with their parents (who are members) and their marriage partners, they form a strong familial stratum that is the main component of the core population, that in itself accounts for about 85% of all those living in a kibbutz. That familial stratum blends with the social stratum to form one large community.

In addition to the strong familial bonds within the kinship group, children growing up together in the kibbutz, which for them is a large shared home, form strong attachments to members of their peer group not unlike their ties to consanguinal kin and often no less intensive. There are signs that the degree of solidarity among second and third generation members who have grown up together, unimpeded by dogmatic ideology that characterized the youth movements in the past, is greater than that found among veteran members held together by a common ideology and comradeship. If so, one can conclude that the kibbutz is becoming stronger as the basis of solidarity shifts from ideological commitment to extended mutual involvement in shared life experiences. Surely some expression of this new reality in which the young grow up must ultimately be framed ideologically, but that shall only further strengthen the process. As that process moves forward, the kibbutz combines within itself what were once thought to be conflicting trends. The familial community combines with what Buber described as Lebensgemeinschaft, with ideological consensus providing a further dimension to social solidarity.

All in all, the kibbutz of today is not breaking up into discrete family units, but rather is welding together smaller social units into a community of a new kind. Earlier predominance of the *meshek* or shared household framework as a source of unity and solidarity provided the conditions for building the community through increasingly broadening and interrelating familial and social networks functioning within a multi-generational framework. The net result is a dialectical connection between the shared household and the community, with the latter developing through a dialectical relationship between familial bonds and comradeship.

Changing Marital Patterns

During the past generation, and particularly since cheap birth control measures have become widely used, there has been a significant change in marital patterns. In post-industrial societies, marriage among women generally has been postponed to the late twenties, and marriage among men generally to the early thirties. In 1989, 34.6% of American women aged 20-24 were married, 62.4% of those aged 25-29, and 71.9% of those aged 30-34. Among American men, 21.4% of those aged 20-24 were married, 49.2% of those aged 25-29, and 66.2% of those aged 30-34.

A similar change in marital patterns has been taking place in the Jewish population of Israel (but not among the Muslims), and in even more extreme form in the kibbutz population as a separate sub-group. As can be seen in the following table, in the years 1961 and 1972 most of the Jewish and kibbutz women were married by age 24, while in 1990/1991 in age group 20-24 only 36.7% of the Jewish women and 11.1% of the kibbutz women were married. However, in 1990/91 among age group 25-29 74.7% of the Jewish women and 65.2% of the kibbutz women were married, and in age group 30-34 the percentage of married women was higher in the kibbutz population than in the surrounding Jewish population.

The census data available for 1961 show a higher percentage of marriage among kibbutz men in all age groups analyzed than in the surrounding Jewish population. The proportions equalized in 1972, and then separated in 1990/91 with more extreme postponement of marriage in the kibbutz population. Among Jewish males, marriage in age group 20-24 dropped from 22.9% in 1972 to 12.3% in 1990, and in age group 25-29 from 71.6% to 53.3%. Among kibbutz males, marriage in age group 20-24 dropped from 22.3% in 1972 to only 3% in 1991, and in age group 25-29 from 71.2% to 37.2%. However, in 1990/91 the large majority of males in age group 30-34 of both population groups were married and the percentage difference between them insignificant (79.9% for Jewish males and 76.2% for kibbutz males).

MARITAL STATUS IN JEWISH AND KIBBUTZ POPULATIONS
(Percentage)

Age Group	Population Group	1961[1]	1972[2]	1990/91[3]
Females:				
20–24	Jewish	64.8	51.9	36.7
	Kibbutz	63.2	50.8	11.1
25–29	Jewish	88.5	82.0	74.7
	Kibbutz	89.1	83.1	65.2
30–34	Jewish	92.5	90.4	84.5
	Kibbutz	94.8	89.6	87.2
Males:				
20–24	Jewish	23.8	22.9	12.3
	Kibbutz	32.6	22.3	3.0
25–29	Jewish	68.3	71.6	53.3
	Kibbutz	77.5	71.2	37.2
30–34	Jewish	85.9	89.4	79.9
	Kibbutz	87.7	89.1	76.2

[1] According to the Population Census of 1961, Government of Israel.

[2] According to the Population Census of 1972, Government of Israel.

[3] Jewish data are for the year 1990, STATISTICAL ABSTRACT OF ISRAEL 1992, pp. 92-93. Kibbutz data are for the year 1991 and refer only to the United Kibbutz Movement (TAKAM).

The most important result of marital postponement is the delay in birth of the first child, and ultimately a decline in the rate of general fertility. In 1965, 42.8% of the births in the kibbutz population were to mothers aged 20-24, and another 29.8% to mothers aged 25-29. Twenty years later, in 1985, 35.9% of the births were to mothers aged 25-29 and another 31.3% to mothers aged 30-34.

AGE OF KIBBUTZ MOTHERS AT TIME OF BIRTH
(Percentage)

Age of Mother	1965/66	1984/85
15–19	6.0	0.5
20–24	42.8	14.3
25–29	29.8	35.9
30–34	13.8	31.3
35–39	6.2	16.0
40–44	1.3	1.5
45+	0.1	0.1
Total	100.0	100.0
Number of Births	1,885	2,869

Source: Central Bureau of Statistics, Govt. of Israel.

In age group 30-34, 87.2% of kibbutz women are married as against 84.5% of Jewish women in the surrounding society and 71.9% of American women. That level is reached among kibbutz men only in age group 35-39, at which stage 87.5% are married in comparison with 89.0% among Jewish men in the surrounding society and 73.9% among American males. Those figures indicate the preference for marriage among kibbutz men and women, despite the prevalent tendency to postpone the time of formalizing the marital relationship and having the first child. Once married, the relationship is usually stable, as shown by lower divorce rates in the kibbutz population as compared with the surrounding Jewish population.

Nevertheless, the prevalent trend of greater mobility among young adults during the past two decades has introduced new elements into kibbutz life, and has made the family less central than it was before. The most dramatic form of mobility has been extensive travels on the part of young kibbutz adults throughout the world. Another form has been the now dominant practice of pursuing higher studies after army service, which keeps both men and women away from their kibbutz for most of the week during a period of several years, and certainly contributes to a delay in the date of marriage.

While the extended family of three or four generations continues to be the standard for most of the kibbutz population, and has been growing stronger despite social and economic changes, it faces serious challenges in the near future. The kibbutz has taken in large numbers of immigrants from the former Soviet Union. During the first stage, the families have been provided with an apartment, taught Hebrew, and given work within a program intended to provide a temporary home during their initial period of adjustment to life in Israel. The program was designed on the assumption that the immigrants would be sceptical about communal living after the disastrous failures in the Soviet Union and the supposedly negative attitude toward the kolkhoz. As it turns out, almost all of them are from the big cities and have almost no knowledge of the kolkhoz. For the most part, they fit into daily kibbutz life with relative ease, but after long years of shortages in more attractive consumer goods it is hard for them to suppress the desire to acquire private possessions, and that makes them strong advocates of consumerism at a time when the kibbutz is struggling to curb consumerist influence.

Presumably, thousands of the immigrants from Russia and elsewhere will become kibbutz members as they move from temporary to permanent settlement. For the most part, they are currently accustomed to small families, but have strong attachments to the wider network of family relatives. From that point of view, they should fit into the familial context of the kibbutz without too much difficulty. The difference in mentality, though, is a source of concern. A particular difficulty is the reported general distrust of those in charge of public affairs, and even of other people who are not part of the intimate circle. Kibbutz life is based strongly on trust in other members, and throughout kibbutz history that trust has been betrayed only in rare instances. Indeed, as the kibbutzim have grown larger, with expansion of the economy and accompanying pressures of consumerism, trust rooted in direct personal relations has had to be attenuated by more formalized relations, and particularly in economic matters. That trend now threatens to weaken both comradeship and familial bonds as market relations penetrate the kibbutz framework.

As shown in previous chapters, that development does not mean a linear movement toward a market society (Gesellschaft), but does indicate that the socioeconomic structure of the kibbutz is going to acquire increased importance in the sense of a communal household. How the young kibbutz adults returning from travels around the world and from professional studies, as well as the thousands of immigrants who are entering kibbutz membership, shall fit into that emerging pattern of a communal household-- and to what extent it shall answer their needs--is a question that shall dominate the 1990's.

Chapter Eight
KIBBUTZ AS A COMMUNAL HOUSEHOLD

For all of human history people have lived in groups of one kind or another. Larger societies have been formed by combinations of such groups interacting within a common framework, and that framework has usually been a political structure of some kind. Until recently, most people have remained for their entire lives within the group to which they had been born. Likewise, most people have remained in the place of their birth for their entire lives. Identity of an individual has come primarily from those two sources: the social group to which he belongs and the place or natural environment of his residence. The repeated resurgence of ethnic identity as a major source of unity in times of crisis demonstrates the enduring importance of relatedness to the primary group over any political or socioeconomic bond.

The individualism and high degree of social mobility that characterize contemporary market societies are a recent innovation, and a direct result of the particular socioeconomic conditions created by an expanding market economy. Capitalist market forces have steadily gnawed away at the familial fabric of society, admittedly leaving most individuals in better material conditions of life but considerably poorer psychologically. Social criticism of the capitalist market system has been continuous and increasingly severe as alienation, loneliness, and mental illness become more prevalent, with their accompanying phenomena of drugs and violence. The fault in the emerging market society is that it increases individual freedom at the cost of destroying bonds with the primary group, and particularly the family, rather than building mutual support among them.

As the world reaches the end of the twentieth century, local and regional markets are being absorbed into a massive global market, dominated more by transnational companies than by national governments. In effect, political forces are losing control of the economy. The social consequences are alarming. On the one hand, a culture of consumerism is being cultivated by sophisticated marketing techniques intended to create demand for products, too often based on irrational rather than rational choice with little regard for actual use value. On the other hand, an increasingly unequal distribution of wealth, along with an exploding population and growing unemployment, leave more and more people frustrated by their inability to afford purchase of those goods and services for which demand has been stimulated. The inevitable result is expression of that frustration and anger through violent demonstrations, vindictive destruction, and forceful possession of consumer items by stealing or looting.

The dominant trend toward urbanization is based on individual initiative to leave the primary group in villages and towns in order to move to the expanding markets in urban centers. More retarded economic development in the countryside (in many countries to the extent that the local economy cannot support the expanding population) means less purchasing power and fewer opportunities to participate in the "culture of consumerism". While deep and even desperate economic need may be the primary driving motive for moving to a city, in the background is a contest between the traditional culture of the locality and the new consumerism.

Purchasing power is a prerequisite for participation in the the culture of consumerism, and the place to get it is in the city. That is also the place where consumerism can be enjoyed at its widest range. More clarification is needed on this subject to distinguish between the quest for income, and its influence on the migration to urban centers, in order to enter the new culture of consumerism as against the quest for income in order to survive along with the traditional culture. Prominent research on urbanization shows both trends at work, with migrants bringing consumerism back to their villages and then a struggle to integrate consumerism and traditional customs.

The core unit being changed is the household. The chief victim is patriarchalism. Previously, the male head of the family was in charge of the household economy and usually the main provider. In the market society the head of the family may be unemployed and economically dependent upon his employed sons, or even on his working wife. Even when the head of the family is employed and provides the main or sole income, most decisions about how it should be spent within the culture of consumerism are not made by him. Typically, the employed provide the income while housewives determine how most of it should be spent. At best, there is a discussion about allocation of resources and an attempt to reach a consensus about what purchases are more important than others. As economic power leaves the sole control of the patriarchal figure and spreads out among other members of the household, so too does authority. A whole new structure of human relations is taking place as a result of these processes of change.

The more important revolution taking place in our time is in the household, and it is in this sphere that the kibbutz is emerging in the 1990's as a creative leader in a new direction. During its evolution, and particularly in the period of the 1960's to the 1980's when large numbers from the second generation entered into membership, the kibbutz succeeded in reestablishing the family on a multi-generational basis. At the same time, the younger members have shown strong inclinations toward individual development and greater individual choice in matters of consumption. Those pressures have shaped emergence of a new household model, based on a large domestic group made up of many families and individuals.

The Household

Households are the basic units of the market economy, and the domestic groups living within them are the cells of the market society. Private consumption of citizens (as distinguished from consumption by government and other public institutions) accounts for most of the Gross Domestic Product of any country. Most of the money spent on private consumption is channelled through the household budget. Therefore, the household and its involvement in the market are of crucial importance for an understanding of contemporary social and economic changes on a global scale. One result has been a new and better understanding of the household, and the changes taking place within it.

There has been considerable confusion about the meaning of household.[1] A commonly accepted practice up to the past few decades was to equate the household and the family. More recently, "household" has come to means a socioeconomic unit were members of the domestic group have a common residence and take a significant part of their meals together. The domestic group may or may not be a family. That definition is now common among demographers and is useful in assembling national statistics. However, it could also be applied to residents of a boardinghouse where people may live and take their meals together in exchange for payment without ever forming a household. The key element missing in the above definition is that a household is formed on the basis of a common purse, into which goes income and out of which comes payment for expenditures. Within a true household, there are no payments or other commercial transactions between members of the domestic group, except through the intermediary of the common purse.

The household income covers needs of all members of the domestic group living within that household. In a more precise sense, the household is not the domestic group and therefore cannot be equated with the family. Rather, it is an economic unit distinct from the social or domestic group that it serves. The members of such a group may come or go, increase or decrease, without changing the continuity of the household. Even in a conventional family household,

----

[1] Donald R. Bender, "A Refinement of the Concept of Household: Families, Co-Residence and Domestic Functions", AMERICAN ANTHROPOLOGIST, February 1967, pp. 493-504; Peter Laslett (editor), HOUSEHOLD AND FAMILY IN PAST TIME, Cambridge University Press, 1972; Sylvia Junko Yanagisako, "Family and Household: The Analysis of Domestic Groups", ANNUAL REVIEW OF ANTHROPOLOGY, 1979, pp. 161-205. N. Keilman, A. Kuijsten and A Vossen (editors), MODELLING HOUSEHOLD FORMATION AND DISSOLUTION, Oxford University Press, 1988. David I. Kertzer, "Household History and Sociological Theory", ANNUAL REVIEW OF SOCIOLOGY, 1991, pp. 155-179.

members may come and go at various times yet the household itself has a continuous existence.

The combined income of the household, from whatever sources, usually is derived from the surrounding market economy. The chief function of the household is to provide at least the essential needs of its domestic group -- primarily food, clothing and shelter -- and usually beyond that in the various forms of care, comfort and leisure. The goods and services acquired from the market by the household through collective purchasing are distributed to members of the domestic group without the household receiving payment in exchange. That is the essential difference between the household economy and the market economy. The household is mainly concerned with distribution of goods and services to the members of its domestic group, and therefore is essentially a **distributive economy**, while the market is based on exchange and therefore is essentially an **exchange economy.**

However, the household also functions as a part of the market and its exchange system. Just as household income is derived from the market economy, so too, most goods and services required or desired by the domestic group come from the market. The household exchanges its income for those goods and services. From that point of view, the household is the economic unit that deals with the market and as such it is the intermediary between the market and the domestic group. In other words, the household economy really serves a dual function. Insofar as it deals with the surrounding market society, it must function in terms of exchange, both in securing income and in dispensing purchasing power. That is its external role. Internally, however, the household is concerned only with distribution.

Much has been made of the apparent contradictions between the household and the market, particularly the pernicious influence of the market in penetrating within the household and eroding its shared consumption from within. Actually, there is a dialectical relationship between the two, with many positive features. As it turns out, most of private consumption is possible only on the basis of shared consumption. Supermarkets or shopping malls are a prominent example. For a maximalization of merchandizing, there has to be a wide range of goods and services. In a parallel way, for a maximalization of private consumption there has to be a wide range of choice. Supermarkets and shopping malls are built on a combination of the two by providing a framework within which many consumers may roam around at their own pace and choose what they wish to buy. That framework, however, is shared territory and without that sharing private consumption could not reach the levels that supermarkets and shopping malls have helped attain. Not accidentally, the merchandizers try to maintain within that shared framework a friendly "home" atmosphere, often with music and skillful interior decorating, and often attractive landscaping. That trend is in contrast to the old image of the market as a place of conflict between economic interests, with strictly impersonal "business" relations.

Even clearer examples can be found in the dependency of private consumption upon shared systems for providing water, electricity, roads, postal services, etc. During the past century, the most important attempts to improve private consumption and personal choice by broadening shared systems have been pioneered by socialism. All of these shared systems are parts of a distributive economy, and that has been the foundation of socialist policy. Meanwhile, most of the distributive systems introduced and developed by socialists, have been accepted as constructive by capitalist market forces and are now part of the general consensus. Indeed, capitalists have often shown more initiative and achievement in expanding shared systems of consumption than have socialists. A prominent example is the rapid expansion of electronic communications in recent years, to the point where the world has been called a "global village". In effect, that is an extension of what began with the postal system.

Many of the proposals for more public facilities and services have been accepted by public opinion as inseparable from enlightened government, particularly free public education, health care, and old age pensions. There are still many die-hard opponents, who hold that the public purse cannot afford the cost of so much support. At the heart of the debate is the question of whether political structures at the local, regional or national levels are intended to function like public households, providing and caring for the residents, or if they are to serve only as a framework for the contest of market forces and interests, without regard for the weaker and more needy. Actually, governments of all kinds are public households, with the main purpose of promoting the well-being of the residents forming the domestic group of the particular government.

Facilities and services provided by any government are forms of collective consumption. Their continual expansion indicates a growing trend toward synthesizing market and household economies by integrating their exchange and distributive functions. Insofar as that trend serves to moderate the more harmful effects of the exchange economy, it moves in a positive direction and helps to close the gap between the household and its surroundings. However, when attempts are made to introduce the exchange mechanism into the household and to impose it on the domestic group, the results can only be negative.

The housewife or other designated person within the household making the purchases is the actor who carries out the transaction and has direct personal contact with the market on a day to day basis. Most of the domestic group do not have such involvement in the market. An exception, of course, is the person or persons who derive the household income by their direct involvement in the market through their place of employment. While such people provide the income, they usually have little to do with expenditures. The relations between income and expenditures are mediated by the household structure, with the various activities distributed among members of the domestic group, and with varying degrees of participation in decision-making about the use of household income.

In former times, the dominant culture of the domestic group was shaped by the distributive character of the household economy. Efforts were made to ensure that neighborhoods and even entire villages or regions would maintain cultural patterns closer to those of the household rather than to those of the market. Good neighborly relations are usually marked even today by rejection of commercial exchange and preference for free giving and taking as within a household.

Distributive and exchange economies in their extreme forms are polar opposites. There is an on-going dialectical tension between them, with the balance shifting sometimes in one direction and sometimes in the other. During the current era, the expanding world market has given enormous power to the exchange economy and its derivative culture of consumerism.

As it turns out, though, consumption cannot be individual and private alone. It depends on the support of collective or shared consumption. Further development of shared systems of consumption is a necessary pre-condition for the expansion of individual choice in private consumption, and these are provided by the expanding world market.

The success of consumerism also depends on the degree to which it is able to influence and direct household expenditures. To achieve this goal, the market reaches inside the household in order to persuade members of the domestic group and to induce demands among them for particular goods and services. This invasion of household privacy is accomplished mainly through advertising. As this process continues to develop, the household becomes less and less of a protective shield separating the domestic group from the market.

Along with increasing emphasis placed on the individual consumer by the advertising media is a parallel demand for more privacy in order to enjoy individual consumption in contrast to the shared (distributive) consumption of domestic or public groups. The appeal to individual consumers encourages smaller domestic groups and ultimately leads to the phenomenon of single person households as the extreme case of individual consumerism, brought almost to the state of cultural autism in the guise of exemplary personal freedom. One of the most significant demographic changes in market societies within the last generation has been the extraordinary growth in single person households among younger people, where the situation is obviously of personal choice and results in making total household consumption equivalent to individual consumption. In the United States, the number of single person households in age group 25-44 grew from 1.6 million in 1970 to 7 million in 1989. There has been a similar process in most European countries and in Israel.

This development is obviously an anomaly at a time when the vital contribution of shared consumption is becoming increasingly clear. The individual consumer in his individual household is dependent upon the collective kitchen of the food-processing plant that prepared his pre-cooked dinner. The television network that he shares with hundreds of millions of other viewers provides contact with the world. He drives his car on roads that he shares with millions of other drivers. He may enjoy sitting on a

80

bench in a public park shared by thousands of others. The idea of completely private consumption, on the basis of completely free personal choice, is as remote from reality as the corresponding idea that a given community can achieve complete autarky or self-sufficiency.

Alongside this trend toward single-person households is another one based on two or more persons forming a shared or joint household for mutual advantage in coping with the culture of consumerism. By pooling their income in a common household budget they are able to maintain a standard of living which they would not be able to enjoy individually. Here the strategy of forming a shared household is used as a means of countering negative influences of the market economy while securing maximum benefits.

From Family to Domestic Group

For many years empirical evidence justified the commonly held belief that the family is the basic unit around which all societies develop. Though families throughout the world have varied considerably in size and internal structure, in all instances they have been formed out of some combination of conjugal and consanguinal relations. The two primary functions of the family have been to provide for the immediate survival of the familial group and, in the long run, to ensure natural reproduction for survival of the larger social or ethnic group. Ultimately the continued existence of the human species is guaranteed by giving birth to children and raising them. In most societies, these two functions still form the center of familial life and they are organized within a household framework.

In view of modifications taking place within the expanding market system, changes have become necessary in the understanding of both family and household. The market economy has influenced a shift in emphasis within the household from production to consumption. As a result, the household in market societies has come to concentrate on serving the ends of consumerism while obscuring the large measure of work still performed at home.

In the past, the domestic group within the traditional familial household usually included members of the immediate family, other residents who might be more distant relatives, and the household servants, though size of the household would usually be determined by economic circumstances. All members of the domestic group had their function, with all able members taking their share in providing for the needs of the group, as well as participating in shared consumption from a common kitchen. In short, they distributed the work and distributed the consumption without trying to connect them by some kind of exchange relation.

The above theoretical discussion provides useful tools for understanding the origins and development of the kibbutz. In the beginning, kibbutzim were formed by domestic groups with no familial ties. The shared household provided the unifying framework, both for work and for consumption. The definitive principle was and continues to be distributive, with both ideological and concrete opposition to market influence. This polarity has been furthered accentuated as members of the group became more and more conscious of the fact that their kibbutz is "home" and not just a transient place of residence. After all, the terms home and market symbolize two very different sets of cultural values and modes of behavior.

In effect, kibbutz members aspired to expand the realm of "home" to maximum limits, even to the exclusion of market contacts. That utopian program for autarky did not succeed. Nevertheless, the kibbutz has gone farther than any other communitarian experiment in history in terms of size and measure of autonomy. All communitarian experiments in the past have been on a smaller scale in terms of combined size and duration. Had the kibbutz been able to get under way a century or two earlier, when industrialization was at a lower stage of development, it might have reached even broader success within a shorter period of time. As it happens, emergence of the kibbutz coincides with expansion of the world market economy, and that has complicated matters for the kibbutz.

Home and Market

For most of human history, there has been a clear distinction between two quite different focal points in the social life of human beings. One has been the private sphere of the home, where people live together in conditions of sharing. The other has been the public sphere of exchange called the market. These two are related dialectically in that they are interdependent although they are quite different. Human life is caught up in the polar dialectical conflict between them, with only utopian visions holding out any hope of overcoming the underlying tensions.

In pre-industrial societies, home and the immediate home environment have been the center of life, with a visit to the market as more of a social event than an economic operation. In industrial and post-industrial societies, the market has come to dominate social life. Market relations and values now determine human behavior to a degree that has proven harmful psychologically and morally. The home, as an environment for the cultivation of inter-personal relations and mutual care, has become in large measure overshadowed by the abstract socioeconomic functions of the household serving as the primary instrument for coping with and adapting to market demands. Conflict between distributive and exchange functions is increasingly a part of home life, with disruptive consequences. Distributive economy has traditionally prevailed in the home as a part of a total commitment to shared life within the family. That is no longer so within the household, where domestic groups are less and less concerned with shared life, as evidenced by the relatively easy and frequent fragmentation of families in market societies.

The market has developed for the purpose of exchange. Goods and services (including labor) are exchanged for mutual benefit. As long as the principle of mutual benefit remained dominant, the market served as a useful social instrument, and even an indispensable one. However, with the emergence of capitalism, profit became the dominant motive along with individual interest in achieving maximum personal gain. That has turned the market into a battlefield of conflicting interests, with modern governments needed in order to maintain an essential measure of law and order within their own territories. More recently, growth of the world market has necessitated formation of international regulatory bodies that already form the nucleus of future world government. Whether it is the marketing of goods, services or just plain labor, past events have demonstrated clearly that there must be some limitations and controls in order to prevent uninhibited greed from nullifying the basic principle of exchange for mutual benefit vital for society's survival.

In advanced industrial and post-industrial societies. capitalist marketing has reached such levels of saturation into every facet of social life that it has become the dominant force shaping the society's culture and way of life. In a certain sense, the market has weakened the "home" and strengthened the "household" by turning the latter into an extension of the market. That part of income which is intended for purposes of consumption is termed a household budget, which then must be used judiciously to answer all or most of the requirements of the domestic group within the household in accordance with economic calculations. Whether in single, familial or any other kind of household, budgeting consumption (including leisure activities) has become a major preoccupation for most people in market societies.

Ernst Bloch has told us that we should continue to hope for a utopian change that shall restore primacy of the home over the market. Some utopians have tried to achieve that goal by detaching themselves from the market through experiments with autarkic communities, but that process is retrograde. *The only constructive way out of the dilemma is by strengthening the household as a protective shield for the home, rather than as an instrument of the market.* The kibbutz is today one of the most successful experiments in that direction so far undertaken, though the problems that remain are still formidable.

The Kibbutz Household

Early kibbutzim grappled with separation of the family and the household long before current trends made the issue an imperative problem. Since founding members of early kibbutzim were very young, and there were in the beginning few cases of conjugal or consanguinal bonds between them, primary emphasis was placed on forming a socioeconomic framework capable of meeting the existential needs of a social group. Work was the central activity, but otherwise life revolved around the shared kitchen and dining hall, which were the social center of the emerging community. Sleeping quarters in tents or wooden huts were a subordinate matter and purely functional.

However, not much time passed before cohabiting couples felt the need for greater privacy in the form of their own tent or room. After that came the children. There were heated debates over the issue of whether the children belonged to their parents or to the community as a whole.

84

An unique compromise was found in a system of collective education, where the children were raised in peer groups and lived in separate children's houses, with daily visits to their parents in the late afternoon and evening. The family remained a social sub-group within the larger community, with all economic relations concentrated in the overall kibbutz household.

For most of the first generation, the dominant policy was anti-familialistic from fear that stronger family bonds would lead to weakening and dissolution of the community. However, an unexpected dialectical process brought about an entirely different result. The shared or communal household arrangements intended to divest the family unit of all economic power, in effect, removed the most serious source of conflict between family members, and left them to concentrate on building strong and enduring interpersonal relations. Furthermore, the communal economic structure proved large enough and flexible enough to absorb all of the young who wish to remain within it.

By 1991, there were 129,300 persons living in 270 kibbutzim. More than half of the young choose to continue in kibbutz life, and now over a third of all members have been born and raised in the kibbutz. They form the second and third generations (and in some cases even the fourth) of extended family units which have come to characterize most kibbutzim. These multi-generational families are the backbone of mature kibbutz communities, and insure their stability and continuity despite economic and other crises which have persistently afflicted kibbutzim throughout their history. It would be no exaggeration to say that the path of the kibbutz has been paved with crises, and that is not unusual in view of the presumption on the part of kibbutz members to go a different way from the surrounding population.

As these familial groups expand, however, the feeling of home changes. In an earlier period, when the kibbutzim were smaller and families were just beginning to emerge, the question of home was muted. For the second generation, there was some confusion in relating to the space within the children's house and the parental apartment as against the entire territory of the kibbutz. By the time the third generation had come along, sleeping arrangements for the children had been shifted in most kibbutzim to the parental apartment which more easily developed as the focal point of immediate human relations, warmth, and love; while the "kibbutz" was becoming ever bigger and more remote from the children. Most kibbutz children now have personal access to the space not only of the parental apartment, but also to that of grandparents and other kin. Within each such space, there is a pattern of human relations that is qualitatively somewhat different from that which prevails in the "kibbutz" space as a whole. For the younger members, the "kibbutz" is increasingly the shared household which functions primarily as a socioeconomic framework.

As a result of changed circumstances, the old pioneering values of the kibbutz connected with self-sacrifice for the common good have ceased to be paramount and have been replaced by cooperative efforts for the common good that is expected to bring better individual well-being. A large majority of the present kibbutz population wants a permanent way of life that lacks nothing of quality in comparison with the surrounding society, while at the same time enjoying the advantages of genuine community within a shared household. How to combine the two is not clear, and there are no historical examples available. A solution has to be worked out pragmatically, without the help of an ideological map or even consensus about ultimate objectives.

The situation requires careful and deep study. Probably at no time in the past have human groups been faced with a comparable situation. Founding members of the kibbutz had a very different view of what the kibbutz ought to be, and did their best to obstruct development in the present direction. The ideological conflict between fathers and sons left scars, and that is an important reason why the present generation is reluctant to adopt a dogmatically ideological position with regard to anything. The kibbutz population is well educated and wants maximum freedom not only for the more banal forms of consumerism but also for consumption of finer cultural products and for personal creativity. In contrast to the older generation, the younger generation has a deep feeling of security and is not afraid that any breach of egalitarian togetherness might shatter the kibbutz. Younger people want more freedom of movement, more individual opportunities in accordance with their own personal traits, and much wider horizons. Since such pressures are clearly at work within the kibbutz, many outsiders find it difficult to understand what continues to hold it together.

No obvious answer, theoretical or ideological, can be given. An examination of the facts, though, shows that a surprisingly large number of the young choose to remain in their kibbutz, and there must be a strong reason for their choice. Statistical evidence to support this contention is given in the appendix. Even among those who do choose to leave, the continuing strong attachment to their kibbutz and the emotions aroused when they revisit, are generally acknowledged. Apparently the system of a communal household has a strong, though as yet insufficiently defined, influence in formation of the individual personality. Whether the current trend toward individualism and greater importance for the familial living space shall change that influence and if so, in what direction, is a subject that should occupy much attention during the coming decade.

According to various sources, the immediate and semi-isolated traditional Jewish community of the Diaspora was regarded by its inhabitants as an extension of the familial home, and especially during the period of the eastern European "shtetl". Today, the kibbutz is not an extension of the familial home. Rather, the expanding familial locus of home (usually spread over several apartments), is an organic part of the kibbutz within an original creation of a new social order. The binding socioeconomic force continues to be the large household framework shared by all members. Clearly, that household framework shall have to prove flexible during the coming years, yet it must retain its overall unity for the system to continue functioning. The natural familial bonds that have developed within that framework have proven to be a powerfully cohesive force.

Tri-part dialectical relations between the household, the domestic group as a whole, and the family units within that domestic group, are now the necessary framework for understanding the contemporary kibbutz and its future. The challenge facing the kibbutz in the 1990's is how to maintain an affirmative balance between the three of them internally, while at the same time working out affirmative relations with the surrounding market society.

STATISTICAL APPENDIX

Section One: General Kibbutz Population

Data in Tables 1-12 are from the Central Bureau of
Statistics, Government of Israel.

Table 1: POPULATION GROWTH

Year	Kibbutzim	Population
1910	First kibbutz founded.	
1950	194	67,539
1960	221	77,955
1970	237	85,100
1980	256	111,200
1985	268	125,200
1986	269	126,700
1987	268	127,000
1988	270	126,100
1989	270	124,900
1990	270	125,100
1991	270	129,300

Table 2: GEOGRAPHICAL DISTRIBUTION (1991)

Kibbutzim are scattered throughout Israel, but most are
located in the northern valleys and Galilean mountains, as
well as in the Negev desert to the south.

Area	Kibbutzim	Population
Upper Galilee	29	14,400
Western Galilee	28	13,900
Jordan Valley	20	10,700
Jezreel Valley	48	28,200
Golan Heights	9	2,300
Central Israel	52	28,400
Judean Hills	8	3,500
Negev	66	26,100
West Bank and Gaza	10	1,800
Total	270	129,300

Table 3: KIBBUTZ POPULATION BY MOVEMENTS (1981-1991)

Movements	Population in 1981	Population in 1991	Net Growth
TAKAM	68,000	78,300	10,300
Kibbutz Artzi	38,000	41,300	3,300
Kibbutz Dati	6,500	8,000	1,500
Poeley Agudat Israel	1,200	1,700	500
	113,700	129,300	15,600

Table 4: KIBBUTZ SETTLEMENTS BY MOVEMENTS (1981-1991)

Movements	Settlements in 1981	Settlements in 1991	Net Growth
TAKAM	161	166	5
Kibbutz Artzi	80	85	5
Kibbutz Dati	15	17	2
Poeley Agudat Israel	2	2	0
	258	270	12

Table 5: SOURCES OF POPULATION GROWTH

Years	Natural Reproduction	Migration Balance	Net Growth	End of Period
1950-1954	10,100	+ 2,500	12,600	76,100
1955-1959	8,600	- 6,800	1,800	77,900
1960-1964	7,200	- 4,200	3,000	80,900
1965-1969	8,700	- 4,900	3,800	84,700
1970-1974	10,300	- 800	9,500	94,200
1975-1979	10,200	+ 1,600	11,800	106,000
1980-1984	10,400	+ 6,300	16,700	122,700
1985-1989	9,600	- 7,400	2,200	124,900
1990	1,500	- 1,300	200	125,100
1991	1,300	+ 2,900	4,200	129,300

Table 6: CHANGES IN AGE STRUCTURE

Age	1948	1961	1972	1983	1991
0 - 14	30.7	34.0	28.7	31.3	28.4
15 - 24	29.5	24.6	23.9	17.6	19.9
25 - 34	20.7	13.0	15.7	16.7	13.4
35 - 44	14.1	10.6	9.1	12.2	13.9
45 - 54	2.7	12.2	8,4	6.9	8.7
55 - 64	0.9	3.4	10.0	6.2	5.6
65 +	1.4	2.2	4.2	9.1	10.1
Total	100.0	100.0	00.0	00.0	00.0
Median Age		21.1	23.9	25.7	26.3

Table 7: KIBBUTZ POPULATION BY PERIOD OF SETTLEMENT (1991)

Period of Settlement	Number of Kibbutzim	Population	Average Size
1910 - 1935	45	33,500	744
1936 - 1949	144	75,300	524
1950 - 1965	32	12,700	397
1966 - 1991	49	7,800	159
1910 - 1991	270	129,300	479

Table 8: CHANGES IN AVERAGE KIBBUTZ SIZE

	1931	1948	1972	1991
Kibbutzim founded 1910-1935	86	625	635	744
Kibbutzim founded 1936-1949	-	-	368	524
Kibbutzim founded 1950-1966	-	-	189	397
Kibbutzim founded 1967-1990	-	-	-	159

Table 9: ALL KIBBUTZIM BY POPULATION SIZE (1991)

Population	Number of Kibbutzim	Percentage	Total Population	Percentage
1,000 or more	10	3.7	12,250	9.5
900 - 999	5	1.8	4,717	3.6
800 - 899	8	3.0	6,647	5.1
700 - 799	21	7.8	15,665	12.1
600 - 699	36	13.3	22,765	17.6
500 - 599	40	14.8	22,215	17.2
400 - 499	43	15.9	19,242	14.9
300 - 399	44	16.3	15,484	12.0
200 - 299	28	10.4	6,334	4.9
up to 199	35	13.0	3,981	3.1
Total	270	100.0	129,300	100.0

Table 10: EDUCATIONAL LEVELS (1990)
(Aged 15 years and over)

Years of Schooling	Men	%	Women	%
0 - 4	100	0.2	100	0.2
5 - 8	2,100	4.6	3,700	8.4
9 - 10	3,500	7.7	3,600	8.2
11 - 12	24,900	55.1	21,300	48.4
13 - 15	11,100	24.6	12,300	28.0
16 +	3,100	6.9	2,700	6.1
Unknown	400	0.9	300	0.7
Total	45,200	100.0	44,000	100.0

Table 11: OCCUPATIONAL STRUCTURE (1990)
(Aged 15 and over)

Occupational Category	Numbers	%
Scientific and Academic	3,200	4.3
Professional and Technical	10,500	14.0
Management	2,600	3.5
Clerical	9,200	12.3
Marketing	2,100	2.8
Services	16,600	22.2
Agriculture	12,800	17.1
Skilled Workers	15,000	20.1
Others	2,400	3.2
Unknown	400	0.5
Total	74,800	100.0

Table 12: EMPLOYMENT BY ECONOMIC BRANCH (1991)

Economic Branch	Kibbutz %	All Israel %
Agriculture	22.9	3.5
Industry & Mining	25.3	21.5
Building & Utilities	0.8	7.1
Commerce, Tourism & Finance	10.9	24.3
Transportation, Communication, & Storage	5.6	6.1
Community Services	16.9	29.6
Personal Services	17.3	7.3
Unknown	0.3	0.6
Total	100.0 74,600	100.0 1,583,100

Section Two: Population of TAKAM

"TAKAM" is the acronym of the United Kibbutz Movement, which includes 166 kibbutzim and slightly over 60% of total kibbutz population. It also includes 7 collective settlements (formerly moshavim shitufiim) that chose to draw closer to the kibbutz model. All data in this section are from the Information Department of TAKAM. There are slight differences between totals because of differences in dates of enumeration.

Table 13: TAKAM - POPULATION

	Mid-1992
Members	36,004
Candidates (Kibbutz Youths)	6,346
Candidates (From Elsewhere)	2,392
Kibbutz Children	24,787
Total Core Population	69,529
Parents of Members	1,101
Other Residents	2,973
Other Children	1,933
Transients	5,222
New Immigrant Adults[1]	1,638
New Immigrant Children[1]	952
Total Periphal Population	13,819
Total Population	83,348

[1] From the former Soviet Union.

Table 14: TAKAM - ORIGIN OF MEMBERS AND CANDIDATES (1991)

	Kibbutz Born	Without Movement Background	From Youth Movement	Other	Total
Men					
18-23	2,986	820	75	179	4,060
24-30	1,464	822	460	140	2,886
31-40	1,609	1,891	900	337	4,737
41-50	1,592	1,585	869	513	4,559
51-65	675	882	1,250	534	3,341
66-100	54	834	1,686	293	2,867
Total	8,380	6,834	5,240	1,996	22,450
Women					
18-23	2,532	841	106	151	3,630
24-30	1,091	1,125	459	118	2,793
31-40	1,328	2,727	621	354	5,030
41-50	1,419	2,066	575	545	4,605
51-65	513	1,169	1,062	469	3,213
66-100	39	1,082	1,910	294	3,325
Total	6,922	9,010	4,733	1,931	22,596

Table 15: TAKAM - PERSONAL STATUS OF MEMBERS AND CANDIDATES (1991)

	Men	%	Women	%
Single	6,864	30.5	5,169	22.8
Married	14,579	64.8	14,747	64.0
Divorced	499	2.2	948	4.2
Widowed	573	2.5	1,820	8.0
	22,515	100.0	22,684	100.0

Section Three: Population of Kibbutz Artzi

All data in this section are from the Department of
Statistics of the Kibbutz Artzi.

Table 16: KIBBUTZ ARTZI - POPULATION

	Mid-1992
Members	19,260
Candidates	3,215
In Army Service	1,870
Kibbutz Children	12,426
Total Core Population	36,771
Other Children	727
Other Adults	1,567
New Immigrants[1]	795
Total Periphal Population	3,089
Total Population	39,860

[1] From the former Soviet Union.

Table 17: KIBBUTZ ARTZI - ORIGIN OF MEMBERS AND CANDIDATES (1991)

	Kibbutz Born	Without Movement Background	From Youth Movement	Other	Total
18-30	2,704	692	743	285	4,424
31-40	1,980	1,336	1,281	260	4,857
41-50	2,069	1,172	1,079	463	4,783
51-65	731	817	1,847	726	4,121
66-100	41	685	3,188	151	4,065
Total	7,525	4,702	8,138	1,885	22,250

Section Four: Population of Kibbutz Dati

All data in this section are from the Secretariat of the Kibbutz Dati.

Table 18: KIBBUTZ DATI - POPULATION IN 1991

Members	2,614
Candidates (Kibbutz Youths)	446
Candidates (From Elsewhere)	143
Other Kibbutz Youths	392
Kibbutz Children	3,209
Total Core Population	6,804
Parents of Members	75
Other Residents	137
Other Children	310
Transients	659
New Immigrant Adults[1]	156
New Immigrant Children[1]	89
Total Periphal Population	1,426
Total Population	8,230

[1] From the former Soviet Union.

Section Five: Kibbutz Industry

Sources of data are the Kibbutz Industries Association and the Central Bureau of Statistics, Government of Israel. Sums are given in fixed prices according to 1991 U.S. dollars. Data for the diamond industry have been excluded since the kibbutz does not participate in it.

Table 19: SALES BY BRANCH 1991

Branch	Domestic Market (%)	Export (%)	Total Sales (US Dollars)
Plastics	62.1	37.9	743,717,000
Metal	63.8	36.2	411,421,000
Processed Food	57.3	42.7	385,647,000
Textiles	67.9	32.1	115,063,000
Pharmaceuticals	86.0	14.0	110,932,000
Construction	98.7	1.3	108,942,000
Printing and Paper	83.8	16.2	107,689,000
Furniture	89.0	11.0	97,364,000
Electronics	69.3	30.7	92,028,000
Optics	49.0	51.0	25,268,000
Jewelry and Crafts	42.7	57.3	12,636,000
Other	100.0	0.0	6,281,000
Total	67.3	32.7	2,216,988,000

Table 20: VALUE ADDED BY BRANCH (1991)

Branch	Plants	Workers	Total Added Value (%)	Added Value per Workday (US Dollars)
Plastics	85	5,865	32.8	166
Metal	83	4,198	32.7	128
Processed Food	28	2,197	22.5	158
Textiles	30	1,090	24.1	102
Pharmaceuticals	18	730	26.4	161
Construction	18	616	32.2	228
Printing and Paper	16	904	27.0	129
Furniture	16	1,360	32.7	93
Electronics	26	1,027	34.0	122
Optics	9	410	44.1	109
Jewelry and Crafts	26	241	26.9	51
Other	11	107	51.4	121
	366	18,745	30.1	143

Table 21: INDUSTRIAL EXPORTS BY BRANCH (1991)
(Millions of US Dollars)

Branch	Kibbutz Industry	Non-Kibbutz Industry	Total Israeli Industry
Plastics	258.8	120.9	379.7
Metal	136.7	813.5	950.2
Processed Food	151.2	386.3	537.5
Textiles	33.9	817.2	851.1
Pharmaceuticals	14.2	1,440.3	1,454.5
Construction	1.3	270.7	272.0
Printing and Paper	16.0	50.8	66.8
Furniture	9.8	41.9	51.7
Electronics	25.9	1,581.9	1,607.8
Other	16.8	928.9	945.7
Total	664.6	7,161.7	7,826.3

Section Six: Agriculture

Data in this section are from the Central Bureau of
Statistics, Govt. of Israel.

Table 22: KIBBUTZ AGRICULTURE (1990)

		Kibbutz	Percentage of Israeli Total
Field and Garden Crops			
Irrigated	(acres)	216,246	49.5
Non-Irrigated	(acres)	123,497	31.0
Orchards			
Citrus	(acres)	10,726	12.4
Other	(acres)	29,859	22.9
Fish Ponds	(acres)	6,756	98.0
Cattle for Beef	(head)	36,157	38.4
Cattle for Milk	(head)	108,506	45.8
Poultry	(tons)	55,636	39.9
Turkeys	(tons)	15,674	28.8
Breeding Eggs	('000 units)	88,842	51.0
Cow's Milk	('000 litres)	477,834	53.1

INDEX

PERSONS:

ORGANIZATIONS:

PLACES: